H~~OW TO~~

RENEW

YOUR LIFE!

This book belongs to

Mary M. Mello

HOW TO *RENEW* YOUR LIFE!

By M. Frazier Keables

1stBooks - rev. 01/28/03

DEDICATION

I dedicate this book to my caring and unselfish Mother, Bessie Pearl (Robinson) Keables Frazier, who set me on the track of investigating and testing many philosophies and religions and the wisdom gathered from civilization's pre-eminent thinkers.

ACKNOWLEDGMENT

Herewith due recognition to my wife, Elizabeth, for her intuitive guidance, her invaluable assistance and her timely suggestions. Her confidence in me is always spurring my latent talents.

PREFACE

Dear Reader:

You may be wondering about all the Fleur-de-Lis emblems appearing on the cover and throughout this book.

According to ancient legend, the Fleur-de-Lis was sent from Heaven to the Frankish King Clovis, the 1st, at the time of his baptism into the Christian Church. Its two "wings" and the one pinnacle are said to represent the Holy Trinity.

King Clovis reigned from 496 to 511 A.D.

Between the time of King Clovis and the reign of Charles the 5th of France (1364-1380), the Fleur-de-Lis appeared prominently in government papers and edicts.

When Charles came to the throne, he designated that the Fleur-de-Lis be recognized henceforth as the Royal Emblem of France.

And, since to the author, the recognition of the Holy Trinity –of God the Father-of Christ the begotten Son-and the Holy Spirit-to be essential to our understanding of the Infinite, it seemed most appropriate to incorporate this insignia herein. Don't you find this bit of history an intriguing romantic touch?

"All the flowers of all our tomorrows
Are in the seeds of today."

B.F.

FOREWORD

This book is not written by a professor, a doctor, a psychologist, or a clergyman, but by a real down-to-earth student of the human psyche.

It is written to reach those of you who have somehow not benefited by the vast numbers of self-help books that are out there now, and for my readers to savor the wisdom of the foremost thinkers of this century and of ages past.

Just what are the arts we need to master for a truly rewarding life?

In random order, they are as follows: the art of communication, the art of making love, the art of sensing another's need, the art of the appreciation of beauty, the art of making others feel at ease, the art of employing our talents to the fullest, and the art of developing our individual worth.

I am sure you would agree that to do these things, even in small measure, would constitute Successful Living.

Inbred in every human heart is the encompassing desire for the better things of life, such as excellent health, a better education, a more adequate home, exciting trips and vacations, and the affectionate love-life of a devoted partner – in other words, the **Good Life!**

Since "God is no respecter of persons," (Acts 10:34), I felt that there was no reason in God's world why I shouldn't experience this kind of life, since I was diligent in work and passionate, if naïve, in my quest for success.

So, now on into the Introduction.......

INTRODUCTION

Not having any illustrious letters after my name, before writing this book, I asked myself, "How qualified am I, and what kind of research can I do which has not already been done, and what additional knowledge could I disseminate which would be of invaluable help to the reader?

In a flash my answer came: I would imbibe the ultimate observations of the greatest Power Thinkers of the world and set down their thoughts in a clarifying and understandable manner. My message would be simple, but eloquent and demonstrable.

Emerson says: *"There is guidance for each of us and by lowly listening, we shall hear the right word."*

At this time you are no doubt asking, "What different noteworthy quality does this book have and just how will it guide me into *my* ethereal Utopia?

Good questions.

There are, of course, numberless and excellent self-help books and tapes in the stores and on the bookshelves, containing an endless variety of wise and witty truisms. One can find any subject discussed from the mystical and the occult to the most modern psychological and philosophical treatises.

When you consider all of the books about happy and successful living which have been published over the centuries, no one could live long enough to digest them all.

How, then, can this book be of as much, or of more value, than others written on the same theme?

You be the judge.

I am not taking issue with anyone whose philosophical system has made anyone rich, or eased the cares of another. Admittedly, they all have a sure-fire course for some. But the big question is: "Will it work for me?"

Many of you have read the glowing testimonials which appear in each of these books. And you feel that you are just as deserving of earth's bounty as anyone else; and unquestionably, you are! (Perhaps even more so.)

The remarkable thing to make clear right now is that "deserving" has nothing to do with it. That is fallacy #1. Get that idea out of your head. No one felt any more deserving than I after working a six-day week, and dedicating myself so diligently to the task that vacations and weekends were practically non-existent!

But calendar years mean nothing in the cosmic plan for success. It is finding the FORMULA which is the trick. And I was determined to find it.

Faithfully did I read and re-read scores of self-help books, the 1st Psalm and the 3rd chapter of Proverbs. Hundreds of affirmations I declared and wrote, visualization I practiced, and actions I took, but withal there was no apparent lessening of adverse conditions.

I am not casting aspersions on any of the books I investigated and studied. They all have a beneficial input for some. Many of the authors are enlightened scholars who have devoted years of research and travel seeking out valuable secrets of the Eastern religions which are not commonly recognized in the West. In Dr. Dean Ornish's best-selling book, *"Reversing Heart Disease,"* ©1990, are some proven Eastern methods of relaxation. But for me the solutions were not there.

As you get into my book, read some of the others which I recommend. You will learn a great deal from them. Set a program of inspirational reading for yourself. It will definitely widen your viewpoints and expand your horizons. Thousands have been successful in using the various techniques presented in these manuals.

But many other thousands have been frustrated and turned off for lack of results. Therefore, I am addressing this book mainly to those of you who have sincerely tried, but found whatever method you have used sadly lacking as a means of redemption for you.

For years I put off writing this book, for I thought that I must have the perfect answer before putting my thoughts into print. I pictured myself writing from a lavish studio, in a comfortable home in the suburbs where I would find much inspiration to write amid pleasant and supportive surroundings.

After many years had rolled by and that didn't happen, I finally decided that I would start writing anyway, while still seeking out the proven principles which would produce a workable formula for a more successful life.

I knew that if I were ever to get this book out of limbo, it would have to be done before I had all the answers. In fact, it would be more valuable that way. Because as my success became more apparent, and as the developmental steps would unfold, then that unfolding would be of much more value to you, the reader.

Only by my life's experience could I hope to make the knowledge in this book of worth to you so that you might profit from it. With this perspective in mind I was ready to proceed. The variety of books, tapes and videos now on the market boggles the imagination. With such a diversity of philosophies and systems presented to an avid public, how is one to know what to choose?

Herein you will benefit not only from the learned observations of ancient and modern sages, but you will also be led to assimilate and to understand the most effective means of living a more purposeful life right where you are now.

Since some of the greatest wisdom is to be found in the Bible, we shall be returning to many of its significant gems as we proceed through each of the following fascinating chapters.

You have now arrived at Port#1. Each port of arrival should bring you a new concept of life.

Open the first chapter with joy in your heart, for a whole new world is opening up for you

Read it! Believe it!

THIS IS YOUR LIFE!

CONTENTS

PORT I

WHAT IS MY PLACE IN LIFE?

What are your thoughts about life in general? How is your personal life adjusting to your present mix of work and play? Are you happy with the work you are pursuing, or your goals in life? Do you have any definite goals? Do you feel that your present circumstances are unrewarding, but you have hope that sometime in the hazy future you will succeed? Do you feel downtrodden, or of little value in the scheme of things? And do you wonder if there is any "scheme" at all to your being here?

If you have troubling questions about any of the above and are seeking acceptable answers, if you are concerned about your limited outlook on life in general, or if you are usually agnostic, pessimistic, or cynical, then this book is for you. Let it work its magic as you glide through the developing pages. Let your consciousness absorb the proven principles working for you, providing you with a more perceptive outlook on whatever you may encounter anywhere and everywhere in this world.

THIS IS YOUR LIFE! …Here and Now!

Your outlook on life, possibly now clouded, will be clarified as we proceed.

As we begin, let's get a hold on our mental adventure. You may not be one who is impressed with theological or philosophical exhortations, but if you are sincere in your quest, I am sure that you will find meaningful enlightenment from reading and absorbing the principles presented in the following pages.

1

Whatever your inclinations, I urge you to read on to find out what the accumulation of this wisdom will reveal to you. However, unlike the philosophies and religions which teach that this mundane life is of little intrinsic value and that the life beyond is the preeminent goal, I want you to fully appreciate the seldom realized, yet illimitable, blessings of your current and conscious existence on this Earth.

Savor as much of this life as you can. Learn to appreciate the fascinating beauty and the perpetual evolution of Nature and to feel the deeper harmony of all related living things. Perhaps the ancient Chinese discipline of Tai Chi Chu'uan, now becoming more popular here, will help you realize your ultimate potential. Whatever choices you make, it is always wise to *"prove all things; hold fast to that which is good."* (St. Paul) We are all involved in the game of life. You want to play it well, and you want to play it to win! To achieve this winning edge, you will need to apply the principles I will give you in this book. I guarantee that if you assimilate even a smattering of the ideas which are to follow, you WILL be a winning player.

In this book you and I are going on a journey of exploration. It is to be a rewarding journey. Together we will explore the eternal Truths. They are Truths which I have found to be of inestimable value. You have no doubt heard about them over the years, but for one reason or another have never applied them to your own life.

Just what are these treasured Truths? How do we sift through so many of the inumerable and visionary platitudes to find the abiding ones—the ones that will be of practical help to us, to me, in my present situation?

Read on to discover these valued treaures.

It is the author's intent to make this an enjoyable and enlightening pilgrimage-a journey into the ports of wisdom, knowledge and understanding. Prov. 1-7 says: ***"The fear of (respect for) the Lord is the beginning of knowledge."*** A good place to start. Since knowledge and wisdom are not the same thing, we will need wisdom in order to impart this knowledge. And in Prov. 4, 7+8 we are reminded that ***"Wisdom in the principal thing, therefore get wisdom, and with all thy getting, get understanding."*** So, not only do we need knowledge, but we need understanding in order to translate that knowledge into wisdom both for ourselves and for others.

In Psalms we are further enlightened as we read that ***"Understanding is the beginning of wisdom"*** and ***"Understanding is a well-spring of life unto him who has it."*** To this we add this other important passage from Prov. 8:36: ***"For whoso findeth me (wisdom) findeth life and shall obtain favor of the Lord. For the words of the Law are your life."***

Just how do we define this indispensable quality of "wisdom?" The dictionary enlightens us in this manner: ***"Wisdom is the knowledge of what is true and right, coupled with good judgment."*** And ***"Wisdom rests in the heart of him who has understanding."*** (Prov.14:33).

So, how do we gain this wisdom which is so essential to our well-being?

Marcel Proust, 19th century French novelist, instructs us thusly: ***"We do not receive wisdom. We have to discover it for ourselves by a voyage that no one can take for us; a voyage that no one can spare us."***

And this is the voyage we are embarking on right now.

As David Starr Jordan puts it in *"The Philosophy of Hope"*: ***"There is no excellence in all this world which can be separated from right living."*** And "right living" is begotten of wisdom.

Let us then begin this unfolding odyssey with a dual inquiry. This two-part question, "What is my place in life?" and "What is the meaning of life?" has baffled every thoughtful individual from time immemorial.

Realizing your purpose here should not be a life-long quest, but for far too many of us it is a hazy target. Finding that mission will give your life the inspired direction it needs.

Comprehending our uniqueness and individuality, we perceive that we have a personal choice to develop our own special place in whatever environment we happen to be in.

Vernon Howard in *"Psycho-Pictography"* directs us to: ***"Make up your mind to enjoy the voyage. Sooner or later your mind will agree that it's a great idea. It's your moral duty to be happy."*** What an innovative concept! Not easy to do, and is it practical?

To reach such a jubilant state, you would need both prayer and meditation.

If we are not used to doing a meditation session (and how many of us are?) it will take a level of faith you may not now have. In the beginning you may not see any benefits. The use of the three P's of diligent Patience, Practice and Persistence will ultimately reward you with incomparable dividends.

I know that you won't follow this discipline unless you are convinced that it has some value for you. In our western culture few of us have ever taken the time to meditate and it is foreign to our accepted way of life.

Perhaps this recent research will help to persuade you. At the University of Miami Medical School researchers have recently found that daily meditation increases the immune cell activity, lowers the blood pressure, slows the heart rate, relaxes the muscles and creates a more balanced hormonal condition. Not bad for a ten minute "break" every day! Now it is being said that meditation even retards the aging process….It behooves you to consider this additional benefit.

There are many methods of putting oneself into a meditative mood. Here is a simple one as outlined by Dr. Robert Anthony in his best-selling book *"The Ultimate Secrets of Total Self-Confidence"* with elaborations by the author:

1. **Sit comfortably relaxed, with your hands upright on your lap with thumbs and forefingers touching, and your eyes closed. (Tai Chi method)**
2. **Gently focus on your breathing, inhaling the positive, healing energy through your nose and into your diaphragm and exhaling the negative energy out through your mouth.**
3. **Calmly observe your breathing, and do not let any passing thoughts distract you from this concentration.**
4. **R-e-l-a-x completely and let go-o-o-o, making your mind as much of a vacuum as possible.**
5. **Now reach out and l-i-s-t-e-n. How many of us really listen? Listen for any flash of insight,**

inspiration or intuition which may come your way. After you have listened intently for several minutes, then:

6. **Visualize and affirm the thing that you want. Picture it as vividly as possible. Then do what will seem utterly unrealistic. AFFIRM that you *already* have it!**

7. **Now comes the most important part. You must thank God for your materialized desire. You must feel genuinely thankful that your desire has already happened and that you are now experiencing the results. This will take an absolute faith. But, doesn't the Bible tell us that *"Before you ask, I will answer?"***

Making contact with your subconscious through deep relaxation and then giving it your visual affirmation is the hardest part of all this. Once you have done so, though, your subconscious must be convinced of your faith in its ability to contact the Superconscious and so provide you with your desire. And the only way to convince your subconscious you are not fooling it is to believe that you already *have* the thing you are asking for.

Taking time to write down your goals, and achieving some of the smaller ones, will definitely aid you in finding your true place in life. *Know* that your true place is a place of happiness, a place of fulfillment.

Motivating your quest can be this verse from Psalm 16:11: *"Thou will show me the path of life, in Thy Presence is fullness of joy; at Thy right hand there are pleasures forevermore."*

"Joy" and *"Pleasures"*—intriguing concepts for all of us!

What a revelation to know that that **Presence** is available to us Here and Now!

To find our rightful place in life requires what most of us are loathe to do, namely INTROSPECTION.

In the ensuing pages you will read of various methods of meditation, as given by recognized experts in the field. I present these to you so that you may profit from those which seem most suitable to your life style.

Richard Shames, M.D. and Chuck Sterin, M.D.M.F.C.C. have published an extremely clear and simple exposition of this discipline and proven methods of application in their book, *"Healing With Mind Power."*

In Dr. Wayne W. Dyer's best-selling book, *"Real Magic"* is this further clarification:

"Learning to meditate begins, like all learning, with a belief, a thought that must originate with you. The thought is simple: 'I believe there is something to this experience of meditation, and I am willing to invest the energy to discover it.' That's it! A simple acknowledgment that meditation, though you may know nothing about it, has some inherent value, and a decision to approach it with an open mind.

In order to create that open mind, contemplate for a moment on the greatest thinkers you have admired. Consider the lives and the advice of these spiritual masters who have been more influential than the billions of other people who have lived on this planet. They all encourage us to meditate—to go within—to seek guidance in the silent, invisible space that resides in all of us. Meditation gives you the opportunity to come to know your individual self. It allows you to empty yourself of the endless hyperactivity of your

mind, and to attain an uncommon calmness. It teaches you to be peaceful, to remove stress, to receive answers where confusion previously reigned, to slow yourself down and ultimately, when you adopt meditation as a way of life, to go to that peaceful place anytime. I do mean anytime! In the middle of a business meeting, in the midst of a tragedy, during an athletic competition-anytime! Meditation can and will help you become your own miracle worker and come to know the meaning of *real magic.*"

To enlighten us even more, Richard D. Mann describes the process this way in *"THE LIGHT OF CONSCIOUSNESS":* "This process of meditation is nothing more than quietly going within and discovering that higher component of yourself. After a while, you will come into direct contact with what has always been a mystery in your life. You will discover that infinite, invisible Intelligence which has always been a part of you and your daily life, but you were scarcely aware of it.

The body seems to be moved, purified, the imagery has an unfamiliar and awesome clarity, the spontaneous registry of what one's life and current experiences all imply at their core may take the form of searing insights. Even the stillness comes as a blessing and a discovery. It becomes a feeling of communing with God-with the encompassing Intelligence of the Universe."

You may be thinking that it will be impossible to find fifteen minutes, or even *five* minutes, in the midst of a hectic schedule, just to be quiet and pensive. But wait...after a little practice, you will find that the positive benefits of this new-found discipline will outweigh the negatives with which you may have associated it in the past.

To start is admirable, but to continue amidst criticism, ridicule, and understandable interruptions, will be the test of your commitment.

As Thomas Carlyle says: *"Silence is the element in which great things fashion themselves."*

Somehow the time will be found, if you persevere. It is never easy to shift gears, or to change familiar habits, to a new way of addressing one's problems or attitudes, but practice and determination will produce unbelievable benefits.

Maybe you feel uneasy about sitting still when there is so much crowding in on you. I know. I was. In our American way of life, constant activity is the popular buzzword. Let me reassure you that nothing bad will happen, if you take those few minutes out of your day. Go in with the feeling that only positive results can occur. As you begin to make meditation a daily habit, you will begin to see little benefits of this proven practice of silently communing with yourself.

Mornings are best for meditation, but not obligatory. Try to use the same chair; you will find that this chair will take on a magnetism for you. Sitting with your feet flat on the floor, and comfortably relaxed, you are ready to indulge your fantasies and start to make them come true.

Proverbs 4:13 tells us, *"To take fast hold of instruction; let her not go; keep her, for she is thy life."*

Being quiet, meditating, and listening to your inner feelings are proven methods for putting you on the right pathway to achieving whatever you really want in life.

It's time to go for it NOW!

Now *is* the time for you to look for the mornings to be brighter when you wake up. Look for more satisfaction from your work, even though at present you may be toiling at an intolerable job. Before you know it, you will find yourself smiling more and the little irritations which are part and parcel of all our lives, will not bother you as much as they did before.

That's a plus, now, isn't it?

Having a purpose in life will give you at once more direction and more balance.

BALANCE!…there's a key word. Whether we think about it, or not, we are balancing things all the time. We are balancing our job against our time off; we are balancing family obligations against individual desires; and we are balancing time for reflection against time for *re-creation*.

Balance is the *key* to a successful life! As we gain a larger perspective, we begin to feel assured that we will not be thrown off balance by minor, or even major, troublesome events.

Since all of us are of differing backgrounds and natures, if you find that meditation is not your cup of tea, then imbibe the lifesaving, invaluable gems you will find here, and put whatever instinctive thoughts you discern from them into action.

There are, admittedly, many methods of achieving success and happiness in this life and I do not even pretend to possess even a goodly portion of the answers. What you have glimpsed in this chapter, and what you will see in the chapters to follow are superlative gleanings from some of the greatest thinkers of all time.

WATCH WORDS

"WATCH YOUR THOUGHTS, THEY BECOME
    WORDS;
WATCH YOUR WORDS, THEY BECOME
    ACTIONS;
WATCH YOUR ACTIONS, THEY BECOME
    HABITS;
WATCH YOUR HABITS, THEY BECOME
    CHARACTER;
WATCH YOUR CHARACTER, FOR IT BECOMES
    YOUR DESTINY."

FINDING YOUR PLACE IS OF GREAT VALUE

M. Frazier Keables

PORT II
Part 1

HOW FAR DO I WANT TO GO?

In changing my concepts about myself, just how far do I want to go?

Most of us resist change. This is perfectly natural. We like the security of established habits and outlook. To counteract this resistance, think of change as adventure, as challenge, as REGENERATION!!!

Do I seriously want to enhance my life-style, or am I content with the way things are?

All of us are in different family situations. Perhaps your time is taken up with household chores or with business commitments. Whatever your circumstances, you will want to suit your goals to your own time and pace. We all have to modify the time and the means to achieving our goals according to our individual family and business demands, all the while shooting for more study and demonstration, within reason, of course.

I am a great believer in putting family first, since strong families are the basis of a strong nation. I would never recommend a program which would alienate husband, wife, or other close associates. The ultimate goal in achieving a more purposeful existence is to always harmonize all things and all people within *your* world.

Are you being pressed with seemingly unsolvable problems right now? If so, try and see into the core of the situation and listen to what this particular problem has to say to you. Then consider the whole picture: To earn a living, are you really engaged in the work you enjoy and for which you feel talented?

Whatever work you are in, try and see in what way you may *use* these unique gifts from God for your own prosperity and success. This is the very first thing one must consider in his quest to find lasting happiness in life.

Gratefulness is a worthy quality to work on.

Here are two examples to set you on course.

It was the custom of Henry David Thoreau, 19th century naturalist and author, to contemplate the GOOD before getting up in the morning, to ponder his well-being, and to look forward to each day in a spirit of thankfulness. It is an established fact that the more good news you tell yourself, the more good things are likely to happen to you.

In her book, *"Simple Abundance"*, Sara Breathnach recommends that you start a daily gratitude journal in which you write down 5 things for which you are thankful that day. Oprah Winfrey guarantees that if you do this for 3 months, you will become an entirely different person.

How about that?

Such a program may be hard to believe right now-even sounding unrealistic. For the present, just indulge yourself in the inspired declarations you find herein and reawaken to a new and brighter panorama.

Always remember that there is a tendency in human nature to become like that which you imagine yourself to be.

Ponder that for a moment, and know that:

"ONLY AS HIGH AS I CAN REACH CAN I GROW

ONLY AS FAR AS I CAN SEEK CAN I GO

ONLY AS DEEP AS I CAN LOOK CAN I SEE

ONLY AS MUCH AS I DREAM CAN I BE."

Reach HIGHER, Seek FARTHER, Look DEEPER,
Dream LOFTIER!

Start ***renewing*** your life right now by challenging your accepted credos and proving if they are worthwhile for you. A little reflection now will save you much heartache later on. Each day can bring you further revelation of your possibilities, if you will let it.

Look at the dawning of a new day as the ***re-awakening*** of your soul.

M. Frazier Keables

PORT II
Part 2

AND WHAT KIND OF DECISIONS DO I WANT TO MAKE TO GET THERE?

Since the decisions we make always govern the kind of life we are to lead, we most certainly should not make hasty ones. However, it seems to be human nature to do so, for we all make implicating decisions early in life which we live to regret later on.

Our decisions can make us, or break us, so it is vitally important that we consider all our decisions. In my own case, at the age of twenty-two, I made a decision which changed my entire life. I did not realize it at the time, and I could not grasp how financially strapped I would be for years to come as a result of this inexperienced judgment.

Here is an abbreviated sketch of how this took place. After working as a downtown store clerk for 3 ½ years, I felt that I was getting nowhere. Finding that my boss was ready to close the store and moving his business to the suburbs, I decided to buy his fixtures and go into business for myself at the same location.

To my surprise, he agreed to this arrangement, and I went home that day with my head full of grandiose ideas.

My unbridled ambition to get ahead in the world had been stifled by the extreme scarcity of jobs available at that time. Held down by my then unrewarding existence, I surely was not making any progress in the direction I wanted to go.

Since I knew all the regular customers at the store, the idea of having my very own business not only seemed to be a smart move, but so filled my emotions that I could think of nothing which could deter me. Vivid in my memory were the prosperity years of '28 and '29 when I had good reason to know that this same store was then making plenty of money.

So, with just $45 to my name, with no advice from my elders, and with no idea of how to raise capital, or to finance a business-but with the optimism of ignorance-I opened the store doors on May 1, 1933.

It did not take me long to find out that my former employer had good reason to move out. This was one of the crucial years of the great Business Depression when we were using *scrip* for money.

Such was the beginning of many heart-rending and desperate financial trials and tribulations which would last for too many of the fifty-three years that my wife and I carried on the business...and all because I made a hasty decision when I was still an impetuous youth.

Despite all the adverse circumstances I was facing, I had the unmitigated gall to think that I could survive in such an unfavorable business climate. Yes, I did survive. A naïve, but absolute faith in God brought me through fire, floods and 5 relocations. A little more thought beforehand, and an elementary understanding of the economic facts of the business world, (and a better knowledge of who I was), would have saved me from years of financial deprivation.

To sum up: ALL of your decisions are supremely important. Whether you realize it, or not, you are making decisions all the time. You are the one who decides whether you will be a couch potato, or whether to improve the precious time you have.

Thus you can see how your decisions do affect your destiny. Would that I had known this in my early youth!

Disraeli, 19th century English statesman, states: *"I do not believe that such a quality as chance exists. Every incident that happens must be a link in a chain."* Your decisions are *your* links in that chain.

Bring this quotation to mind when you are at loose ends, or if you feel that your life has no objective or definite place.

Ask the Universal Consciousness (and search within yourself) as to what your mission should be, and when you sense that intuitive flash, put that mission to work with an encompassing passion. Put some **fire** in your **desire** and life will begin to **glow** for you.

Now let your thoughts be anchored to this following proposition:

THERE'S ALWAYS A WAY!

When discouragement knocks at your door, **KEEP ON!**
When fear and failure stare you in the face, **KEEP ON!**
When your hope looks hopeless, and every door seems closed, there's always a way. **KEEP ON!**
When desperate want and need fill your nights and your days, **KEEP RIGHT ON!**

When your best friends turn cold and your enemies get bold, there's always a way. **KEEP RIGHT ON KEEPING ON!**
When injustice and condemnation take their turn, **KEEP RIGHT ON!**
When libel and slander attack you with anger, there's always a way. **KEEP RIGHT ON KEEPING ON!**
When you know you are right, as God sees the right, **KEEP RIGHT ON!**
When success starts to break, and they all say, "You're great!" For God's sake, don't stop. **KEEP ON!!!"**

LIFE-REWARDING DECISIONS ARE ENERGIZING

PORT III

CREATURES OF HABIT

"Wherein thou judgest another, thou condemnest thyself, for thou that judgest doeth the same things."

-St Paul

Don't we find this to be all too true?

Visualization and affirmations are essential requirements for breaking counter-productive habits. Seeing yourself as you want to be is the image you want to project.

Can we even begin to realize how much we are creatures of habit? This lifelong process is so automatic and so stealthy that I am sure that most of us do not.

Almost from infancy, we begin to develop certain "traitorous" habits. These behavior patterns become such a part of us that they are difficult and seemingly impossible to change. But, let us remember that our true nature is God-like – an elevating thought which will inspire us to contemplate this bona-fide, if elusive, image of ourselves.

It follows logically then that we should throw out whatever habits we have acquired along life's way which do not fit the life character we want to become. It has been scientifically proven that it takes at least 21 days to break, or change, a habit-perhaps longer if the characteristic tendency is deeply ingrained. Since we are all actors on the stage of life, we must use our imagination to feel that we are *already* that person we want to become. As we pursue this goal relentlessly with faith and determination, we will find that all of a sudden we have discarded that faulty trait which has beset us for so long.

21

With a new image and a new awareness, we can break these self-defeating behavior patterns. With a goal we can believe in, and a goal we can focus on, our inspiration will give us the necessary drive to overcome any lethargy.

As Thomas Carlyle points out: *"Change indeed is painful, but ever needful."*

And remember, *"When patterns are broken, new worlds can emerge."* –Tuli Kupferbeerg, author of *"Times Change."*

How do we start to change these unwanted habits? Take one habit at a time and decide on some specific steps you will take to eliminate it. Write this down and refer to it daily.

As an example, here are some remedies I would recommend to combat some common communication habits:

1. HABIT: Clearing my throat before speaking.

REMEDY: Speak immediately (and go light on dairy foods which cause mucus).

2. HABIT: Speaking in a raspy, or non-melodious, voice.

REMEDY: Be more conscious of the way you talk, and picture yourself as sounding more mellow. (A tape is extremely helpful in bringing about this change. As one local singing teacher succinctly put it: *"For better enunciation, concentrate on lips, teeth, tip of the tongue."*

3. HABIT: Not listening intently. (Many of us are guilty of this).

REMEDY: Look directly at the person speaking, and concentrate on non-distractional listening. It is rude not to give the speaker your full attention anyway.

4. HABIT: Not taking a genuine interest in what the other person is saying, and pretending to understand even when you don't.

    REMEDY: Even though you do not agree, or fully understand, listen well to his, or her viewpoints. This is not only basic courtesy, but in doing so you might just learn something new.

5. HABIT: Not being confident of your own opinions, or the best way to express them.

    REMEDY: Have confidence that your opinions are just as valuable as the next person's and back them up with facts.

6. HABIT: The extremely common habit of defending oneself, or one's actions, no matter what.

    REMEDY: Laugh it off, or make light of the criticism. Such a response will enhance your invulnerability.

7. HABIT: Answering automatically without forethought.

    REMEDY: Take time to pause and think before answering.

8. HABIT: Interrupting the speaker with the expression of your own thoughts before this speaker has finished.

    REMEDY: When you are in a group of born talkers, it takes a lull in the conversation to wedge your viewpoint in. Not easy to do, but respectful.

9. HABIT: Picturing yourself as ever-forgetful or absent-minded.

    REMEDY: Practice remembering some small things and never say: "My mind is like a sieve."

10. HABIT: Customarily criticizing, or bringing a negative response to another's viewpoints.

    REMEDY: See if there are some positive aspects to this person's opinion.

From time to time, you may have to reinforce your determination to change with a strong affirmation, such as: *"I have the ability. My faith in God releases the power which enables me to do it, or to make it happen,"* or *"I can do all things through Christ who strengthens me."* Believe in your new self. Belief and visualization are the key factors in bringing about a change in yourself.

Resolve now to make no more 'value judgments' regarding your own, or other people's habits.

To aid your endeavors, here are a few helpful suggestions: Make very short term goals-something you can reach right away without too much effort. Success in a small way will give you the impetus to attempt bigger things. For a man, this might mean hanging his neckties up, or putting the toilet lid down. (Nobody wants to look at the water in the toilet. Would you want your child, or pet, to drink that water?) Do anything to make yourself, or someone close to you, a little happier. Sometimes it doesn't take much-perhaps something as simple as relinquishing your monopoly on the T. V. remote control. Just a little thoughtfulness. How much more exuberant a world this would be, if we all trained ourselves to *happify* the life of our family and friends!

Now, ask yourself this: "What habits do I want to discard in order to achieve my short term goals?

"Don't look at the loss of a habit, or a way of life, as the end of the road; see it instead as only a bend in the road that will open up all sorts of interesting possibilities and new experiences." Mary Pickford, movie star of the twenties and thirties.

Here is a quote to reflect on at this time: **"Nothing in the world can take the place of persistence. Talent will not; nothing is more common than unsuccessful men with talent. Genius will not. Genius is almost commonplace. Education will not; the world is full of educated fools. Persistence and determination alone are omnipotent. The slogan, "Press on" has solved, and will always solve the problems of the human race."**

The indomitable Alsatian missionary, doctor and musician, Albert Schweitzer, tells us: *"The great secret of success is to be never used up."* (And from his prodigious life work, he seemingly never was).

When asked for a practical solution to the problem of living, psychoanalyst Erich Fromm came up with this wisdom: *"Quietness. The experience of stillness. You have to stop in order to change direction."*

As you consider this, it is good to ask yourself this question: What are my most important priorities anyway?"

Again, remember:

"WE SOW AN ACT, AND WE REAP A HABIT;

WE SOW A HABIT, AND WE REAP A CHARACTER;

WE SOW A CHARACTER, AND WE REAP A

DESTINY."

BELIEF IN YOURSELF *RENEWS* YOUR SPIRIT!

M. Frazier Keables

PORT IV

USING WHAT IS AT HAND

Now it is time to look for those elusive attributes of Being which are not readily apparent to most of us, but which we will discover as we read on. Let us keep an open mind, alert to any and all revelations which may enter our consciousness at any time.

Let us start with whatever faith we have and to use what is at hand. St. Catherine of Sienna, 14th century mystic and prolific correspondent, observes: ***"To a brave man, good luck and bad luck are like his right hand and his left hand. He uses both."***

It is never easy to do, but let us seek to make the so-called "bad" luck work for us, instead of against us, in transforming problems and mistakes into opportunities.

To quote Dr. Anthony: ***"It is one thing to be dissatisfied with your environment, and another thing to refuse to use it to your advantage. The thing that causes our unhappiness is this: 'We will not use today because it does not suit us. This resistance to reality utterly paralyzes our power."***

He continues: ***"You gain immediate power to change your circumstances when for just one day you act with force on a situation in which you find yourself, whether you like the fact of it, or not. Think of yourself as standing on a step of a flight of stairs-in order for you to get off that first step, you must use it for the purpose of moving off it."***

In much the same vein, Wm. E. Edwards of *"Ten Days to a Great New Life"* reminds us; **"This is where I am today; my only salvation lies in action where I am.**

After this assertion, things change fast. The only action that can start you off to a 'great new life' is the engagement of ourselves with the job at hand. The only life one can know is Here and Now! Hopeful goals for the future rise rapidly out of Full Engagement with the Present."

From Margery Wilson in *"Double Your Energy and Live Without Fatigue"* comes this observation: "Whenever you need anything, say to yourself: 'What have I in the house?' There will be some talent, some value, some service you can render, something you can create. Anyone who is alive is in touch with the great allness of Mind, and some evidence of It in him, or herself, or around him or her, can be multiplied to meet his or her need.

It is not necessary to go anywhere, or to find something or somebody new. What you now have in yourself and your environment is as potentially divine as anything else. Act upon this divinity; lay hold of it, claim it, articulate it, and use it."

If we diligently look around us, we can all find something in our present set-up which we can use to better ourselves. LOOK! ACT! Don't be deterred by what appear to be obstructive appearances.

Whatever you do, *enjoy* doing it. Do it with your whole heart and make it fun! You will find that you will do it better and with less effort.

The Greek stoic Epictetus has said: **"Men are disturbed not by the things that happen, but by their *opinion* of the things that happen."**

Hugh Mulligan puts it this way: **"What I do today is important because I am exchanging a day of my life for it."**

And Dr. Ralph C. Smedley, founder of Toastmasters International, profoundly advises: **"Purpose determines the goal, marks the path, and furnishes the motion power."**

From Charles de Gaulle, revered hero of World War II and two term president of France, comes this wisdom: **"Difficulty attracts the man of character because it is in embracing it that he realizes himself."**

Like sprouts pushing their way up through the earth, we cannot grow without challenges. To enhance what is "at hand" is your own intuition, this indescribable gift, so subtle, so indefinable, and yet an endowment so close to our hearts. If we have not listened to this faculty for years (outside of maybe playing a hunch or two) then we've never truly tuned in to the potential of this powerful "mover and shaker"-our gift from God. As we learn to listen and rely more on this instinct, then we will begin to see the defining and resolution of the things which are close to our hearts.

Ralph Waldo Emerson enlightens us with this: **"All our progress is an unfolding like a vegetable bud. You have first an instinct, then an opinion, then a knowledge, as the plant has root, bud and fruit. Trust the instinct to the end, though you can render no reason. It is vain to hurry it. By trusting it to the end, it shall ripen into truth, and you shall know why you believe."**

As you hold a steady vision of your goals, you will find your intuition coming more and more into play.

Norman Vincent Peale, the famous "Positive Thinking" author, and minister of the Marble Collegiate Church for an unprecedented 52 years, gives us this hopeful dictum: ***"With the creative force of belief, you stimulate that*** *particular gathering together of circumstances which brings your cherished wish to pass."*

Perhaps, like me, you have attended lectures on self-help psychology, or success techniques, and have picked up an idea, or two, which you have tried to incorporate into your own personality. Maybe you have tried Dale Carnegie, or Toastmasters International, to give you new confidence in meeting people and to develop a new awareness of your own capabilities. These courses, and similar ones, are all excellent and are to be praised, but unless we consistently practice and use the principles presented, we gravitate backward into our old habits of timidity and stagnation.

Therefore, if we are not in the frame of mind to utilize the principles we ingest, then again we seek the easier road. We must give ourselves the time and opportunity to follow through on the essentials we have learned in order to achieve our desired objectives.

Are we aware that *"There exists in the structures of every one of us a phenomenal resiliency that allows us to face up to all kinds of physical and mental disorders?"* So says Rene Dubois (Rockefeller University scientist acclaimed for his biomedical research).

Remember that *"Man is harder than iron, stronger than stone, and more fragile than a rose."* (old Turkish proverb, showing how resilient, yet how fragile humankind is).

We must work with what we have, no matter how little we seem to possess. I do not know your situation, as you do not know mine, but each of us has to face up to whatever circumstances life has dealt us. Many of us have not been dealt what would be considered a winning hand. Therefore, we must use whatever talents we have to reverse the negatives in our life and to embellish our own self-esteem.

Now lift your spirits with this quote from William James: *"The grandest use of life is to spend it for something that will outlast it."*

From a Chinese proverb comes this ancient wisdom: *"The gem cannot be polished without friction."*

In similar vein, Justice Oliver Wendell Holmes gives us this balanced observation: *"What lies behind us, what lies before us, are small matters compared to what lies inside us."*

Let's begin now to discover what really "lies inside."

And remember: *"So nigh is grandeur to our dust;*
So near is God to man." (Emerson)

REFRESH YOUR THINKING

THIS IS YOUR LIFE!

M. Frazier Keables

PORT V

TIME

Some of us have more money than others. Some of us have more cars; and some more intelligence and ambition. But, there's one thing of which we all have the same amount.

And that is – TIME!!!

How we employ that time determines to a great extent our success, or failure, in this world of ours. Purposelessly "lazying" away our time won't "cut" it, for *we do not have that much time*!

Kay Lyons of *The Catholic News of N.Y.* makes this observation: *"Yesterday is a cancelled check; tomorrow is a promissory note; today is ready cash – use it!"*

And 18th century German poet, novelist and dramatist, Johann Wolfgang von Goethe imparts this truth: **"Nothing is worth more than the value of a new day!"**

Remember, **"You will never "find" time for anything. If you want time, you must *make* it,"** says Charles Buxton, English author.

A bit of philosophy from W. Heartsill Wilson reinforces this fact: **"This is the beginning of a new day. God has given me this day to use as I will. I can waste it, or I can use it for good. What I do today is important, because I am exchanging a day of my life for it. When tomorrow comes, this day will be gone forever, leaving in its wake something that I have traded for it. I want it to be gain, not loss; good, not evil; success, not failure; in order that I shall not regret the price I paid for it."**

To quote our Dr. Anthony again: **"When you snatch the whip of hurry from the hand of time, you will retain self-mastery. The secret of winning is beginning. Given the emotional motivation to take command, the mechanics of achievement will follow. And most of all, expectancy will set in motion a mighty power within you that will cause your desire to happen. To the creative mind, one moment is exactly like another. Each minute is rich with promise, if we could only but see it."**

Again in *"Double Your Energy and Live Without Fatigue"* Margery Wilson advises that we ask ourselves this question: **"Since when did a clock (a bit of machinery invented by the mind of man) gain ascendancy over me? That clock is there for the order of my life as a convenience, not as a whip or a master. I am master of that clock. If I find pleasure in my day's work, I shall gain energy from it."**

Are you always in a hurry, like most of us – caught up in the popular frenzy? Has it become such a habit that you don't even realize it? If so, you would profit by reading *"What's Your Hurry?"* by Elizabeth Berg, a short classic appearing in the September '93 *Reader's Digest,* condensed from *"Woman's Day"* magazine. You will also be able to find this in paperback.

Pause here and ask yourself: "Am I too busy to discern the unrealized vividness of life which is all around me?"

An ancient Chinese proverb offers this: ***"Someone riding a horse cannot appreciate the flowers."*** If we are in too much of a rush, we will miss those intrinsic values which would otherwise enhance our lives.

Benjamin Elijah Mays puts it lightly in this manner:
**"Life is just a minute, only sixty seconds in it;
Forced upon you; can't refuse it.**

Didn't seek it, didn't choose it;
You must suffer, if you lose it.
Give an account, if you abuse it;
Just a tiny little minute, but *Eternity* is in it."

So, how shall we use this parcel of time allotted to us?

Whether we realize it, or not, we all seek fulfillment. The most important question is how to use this quality of time to bring us the satisfaction of accomplishment. That accomplishment – even the push toward it – will give us that important lift we need to embellish our life.

Here is wisdom for all time: **"Have a time and place for everything and do everything in its time and place; and you will not only accomplish more, but have far more leisure than those who are always hurrying, as if vainly attempting to overtake the time that had been lost."** – So says Tryon Edwards.

The stark reality is that most men live lives of 'quiet desperation.' This word "desperation" comes from the Latin word "desperare", meaning "to be without hope."

Although it cannot be said that the majority of us are not living exactly without hope, yet it is 'hope deferred.' Always not quite comprehending the present, but ever gazing upon that hazy, indefinable future which we never seem to reach. The answer to this interminable frustration is best answered by Jesus in John 10:10: ***"I have come to bring you all the fullness of living."*** "Fullness of living" means living in the NOW!

Don't give up your dreams or your goals. These are vitally important to spur you on to greater accomplishments. Just don't let those future dreams so encompass you that you do not recognize current opportunities.

Try to feel yourself connected to Jesus. As you do, you will begin to sense the unique emancipation engendered by your discernment of the full meaning of the above quotation. Divide your goals into short and long range attainments. *"Study as if you were to live forever. Live as if you were to die tomorrow."* Isidore of Seville, 6th century Spanish archbishop and historian.

By having read thus far, you have already given some needful direction to your life. But you need more, much more to accomplish what you want to do here. Most of us are like flotsam and jetsam on an angry sea with no specific destination in mind – just a general on-the-go outlook. In this kind of dilemma we waste many hours and days actually going nowhere. Such a limited and purposeless perspective leads eventually to frustration, disappointment and despair. To offset this kind of malaise, garner in the wisdom presented by the Power Thinkers in this book and life will take on a new meaning for you.

It will help you to fathom the eternality of life by realizing that, *"The measure of life is in its excellence, not in its length of years."* So stated Plutarch, the eminent Greek biographer of the 1st century A.D.

"Therefore: Look to this day!
For it is Life, the very Life of life;
In its brief course lie all the verities and realities of
your existence:
The bliss of growth, the glory of action;
The splendor of achievement.
For yesterday is but a dream
And tomorrow is only a vision,
But today well-lived
Makes every yesterday a dream of happiness,

And every tomorrow a vision of hope.
Look well, therefore, to this day!"
                                        -from the Sanskrit.

Here's another elevating observation from Andre Maurois, French biographer and novelist: "**Life is too short to be little. Here we are on this earth, with only a few decades to live, and we lose too many irreplaceable hours brooding over grievances that, in a year's time, will be forgotten. No, let us devote our life to worthwhile actions and feelings; to great thoughts, real affections, and enduring undertakings; for life is too short to be little**."

In 1613, Sir Thomas Overlong, author of several monumental works, reemphasized this viewpoint with: "*To live long is to fill up the days that we do live.*"

Pablo Casals gives us his view of the wonder of life, thus: "**Each second we live is a new and unique moment of the universe, a moment that never was before and never will be again. And what do we teach our children in school? We teach them that two and two makes four and that Paris is the capital of France.**

When will we also say to each of them what they are? We should say to each of them: 'Do you know what you are? You are a marvel. You are unique. In all the world, there is no other child exactly like you. In the millions of years that have passed, there has never been another child like you, and look at your body-what a wonder it is! Your legs, your arms, your cunning

fingers, the way you move. You may become a Shakespeare, a Beethoven. You have a capacity for anything. Yes, you are a marvel. And when you grow up, can you then harm another who is, like you, a marvel? You must cherish one another. You must work-we must work-to make this world worthy of its children.'"

Here you begin to glimpse the unity of the Universe and to learn that reverence and respect for all living things are essential elements of becoming a true citizen of this world; and that how you use your time not only has a vital effect on you, but also upon your fellow man.

As Socrates put it so long ago (and what world peace there would be, if we could only all realize it) *"I am not an Athenian, or a Greek, but a citizen of the world."* Amen.

As a world citizen, then, your time here is extremely valuable, even having a unique value you may never have imagined before.

Lord Chesterfield, British statesman and author, (1694-1773) admonishes us in this fashion: *"Know the true value of time; snatch, seize, and enjoy every moment of it. No idleness, no laziness, no procrastination; never put off until tomorrow what you can do today."* (I am sure that we have heard that last phrase many times before).

The immortal Shakespeare tells us: *"O call back yesterday; bid time return."*

But it won't and never will.

So, let's live fully each day as we are able, and not worry about the future, for the past is gone; all we really have is the NOW, the PRESENT!

"Dost thou love life? Then do not squander time, for that is the stuff life is make of." Benjamin Franklin in *Poor Richard's Almanac.*

THEREFORE, YOU SHOULD:

Take time to think....it is the source of power.

Take time to play...it is the secret of perpetual youth.

Take time to read...it is the fountain of wisdom.

Take time to pray...it is the greatest power on earth.

Take time to love and be loved...it is a God-given privilege.

Take time to be friendly...it is the road to happiness.

Take time to laugh...it is the music of the soul.

Take time to give...it is too short a day to be selfish.

Take time to work...it is the price of success.

Take time to save...it is the foundation of your future."

What better creed can you find than that???

Tucked away in our subconscious is an idyllic vision. We see ourselves on a long trip, a trip which, perhaps, spans the continent. We see ourselves arriving at the station, the achievement of our goal. But, sooner, or later, we will realize that there is no station-no one place to arrive at once and for all. The true joy is the trip and not the destination which is always outdistancing us. Let us realize with Sidney Greenberg that *"Life is a journey, not a destination; and happiness is not "there", but "here" and not tomorrow, but today!"*

Relishing the moment and acting on it is an excellent motto, especially when it is coupled with Psalm 118:24: *"This is the day which the Lord has made; we will rejoice and be glad in it."* Let this declaration be your guide every morning of your life.

After all it isn't the burdens of today which drive us mad. It is the regrets over yesterday and the fear of tomorrow which are the twin thieves that rob us of today's potential.

So, stop pacing the **aisles** and counting the **miles**. That nebulous "station" will come into view all too soon.

In the meantime watch more sunrises and more sunsets and revel in the glories of nature.

This day is life's magnificent gift to me!

RENEW YOUR LIFE!

HERE   AND   NOW!

PORT VI

THE IMPORTANCE OF ATTITUDES

Basic to all success books published is the directive that we be positive. How do we develop this requisite disposition? We do it primarily by asserting a truth until we believe it convincingly. If repeated often enough and convincingly enough, the subconscious will believe it. As the subconscious mind accepts this directive, then it will begin to carry out our wishes for betterment.

Really? Then why isn't this happening?

Together let's examine the essential requirements.

In her book *"Personal Power Through Awareness"*, Sanaya Roman declares: ***"A positive attitude must be nurtured until it becomes a natural part of our Being. You can change the energy between yourself and anyone else by using positive words."***

Again, why is developing and maintaining a positive attitude so important? Because a positive attitude produces results, and positive results are what we want and need.

And listen to this author: ***"If there is a positive attitude in focus, you will increase it every time you concentrate on it."*** Murdo MacDonald-Bayne in *"Heal Yourself."*

States William James, the progenitor of modern self-help psychology: ***"Human beings can alter their lives by altering their attitudes of mind."***

Because of the still many monotonous and repetitive things you have to do, does life still seem to be pretty dull, as it does sometimes for all of us? If so, then recharge your batteries with JOSIE.

These five letters stand for **Joyfulness**, **Optimism**, **Spontaneity**, **Inspiration** and **Enthusiasm**. As you begin to picture yourself expressing these qualities, dullness will then start to exit from your life. It has to. The mental image must precede any expected transformation.

Josie was the name of a poodle puppy I used to know. Just for fun, picture yourself as this poodle puppy with all the animation that image would bring! Universally our lives are so structured that we are afraid to break loose – to look at ourselves with a detached perspective – an accomplishment not easily attained by most of us. That detached perspective is the necessary prerequisite to a realistic objectivity.

As much as you can, eliminate needless routine. Routine dulls our viewpoint on life and ages us faster than we would otherwise. To sense the true emotion of *joy*, (so necessary for optimal happiness) we need to develop the rare qualities of the adventuresome spirit, the desire to try something unproven, something new.

As with any positive quality, if you don't feel it, *pretend* that you have it and it will eventually become a part of you.

An attitude of thankfulness will do wonders in changing your outlook. Perhaps you feel that you have nothing to be thankful for. If that be the case, consider your incredible, flexible body, your illimitable mind, and the very fact that you arrived here at all amid the million and one chances that the union of sperm and egg would even coalesce!

Thinking along in this fashion will give you that needful lift.

On the back cover of Dr. Wayne Dyer's book, *"Real Magic"* is this compelling statement: **"Spend some time every day in awe – total, complete awe. Be thankful for**

your liver, your hands, your invisible, incomprehensible, awesome mind. Treat all life with reverence and awe and know that it is all working purposefully. A few minutes a day in total awe will contribute to your spiritual awakening faster than any metaphysical course." Reflect on this viewpoint often.

Can you think of Jesus as being less than positive? NO! He knew whereof He came and He knew his mission on the earth. Few of us can be as assured in temperament, or in character, as He.

I remember talking with a man who had been put in a concentration camp during World War II. I asked him, "Could you still thank God when you were in such an intolerable situation?"

His answer was very positive. "Yes, of course. I still thanked God even though I could not see any way out of my predicament at the time." (This is the key).

His faith finally brought him freedom and to America. What a marvelous demonstration of unswerving faith!

In his pace-setting book, *"You Have One Life-Give It Your Best Shot"*, Richard S. Clarke says: *"Your life should become a constant paean of thanksgiving."*

How significant!

An attitude of gratefulness will do wonders in helping you to become more positive. Why not start right now to thank your Creator for this incomparable blessing of life? *"Joy is to behold God in everything,"* says Julian of Norwich.

Listen to these words from Marcus Tullius Cicero, Roman statesman and orator: *"A thankful heart is not only the greatest virtue, but the PARENT of all other virtues."*

Did you ever consider this ineludible connection before?

Someone has said, **"When our attitude is right, our abilities reach a maximum of effectiveness, and good results inevitably follow. Those who harbor second-best attitudes are invariably second-best doers."**

Could this be true?

The great Albert Schweitzer has this to say about attitudes: *"The greatest discovery of any generation is that human beings can alter their lives by altering their attitudes."* What a seemingly simple thing to do to achieve such far-reaching benefits!

And the Rev. Charles Swindoll, popular Christian author and senior pastor of the First Evangelical Free Church in Fullerton, CA (whose sermons have been broadcast around the world) brings home the significance of this attribute even more in the following passage taken from *"Strengthening your Grip":* **"Attitude is more important than money, than circumstances, than what other people think, say, or do. It is more important than appearance, giftedness, or skill! It will make, or break, a company, a church, or a home.**

The remarkable thing is, we have a choice every day regarding the attitude we will embrace for that day. We cannot change our past. We cannot change the fact that people will act in a certain way. We cannot change the inevitable. The only thing we can do is play on the one string we have, and that is our attitude."

It is time to learn that *"Nothing else matters much, not wealth, nor learning, nor even health – without this gift of spiritual inspiration to keep zest in living."*

We must always remember that our concept of ourselves has a great deal to do with the way we feel. In William Makepeace Thackeray's words: *"The world is a looking glass and gives back to every man the reflection of his own face."*

According to John Stuart Mill, (1806-1873) famous English philosopher and economist: *"Nineteen-Twentieths of mankind unquestionably exhibit a gloomy attitude most of the time."*

DO YOU GET THE PICTURE?

To counteract this negativity, we need to know that *"The measure of mental health is the disposition to find Good (God) everywhere."* (Ralph Waldo Emerson).

Margery Wilson, in her fascinating book, has this to say: **"Unless you are paid handsomely, you will find that devotion to whatever is wrong an expensive hobby. #1. It keeps your mind off the bright and the right, which you need. #2. It prevents the flow of good to you and kills it on contact. 3. It estranges people and kills their faith in your loyalty."**

Muse on the following from *"Cultivating a Happy Mind"* by Susan Valaskovic of the Scripps-Howard News Service: **"Focus on what can go wrong in your life, and it usually does. Look for the good-staying on what is going right – and life improves dramatically.**

You create much of what happens to you by your interpretation of what's going on around you. Negative thoughts alienate you from the one you love, and life becomes the pits.

Of course, there are times in life when something has happened, and sadness and grief are appropriate. But negative attitudes don't usually have a lot to do with a significant event. They are the result of how one

handles the hundreds of situations encountered each week from broken cars to missed meetings.

Staying positive, keeping the heart open, is like maintaining ideal weight. Not only do we need to exercise, but also eliminate those things from the diet that pull the attitude down. Those things include:

GOSSIP: Bathing the mind in gossip is a lot like taking a shower in sewer water. You should change the subject when someone starts gossiping, and avoid those people who insist on doing it around you.

FEAR AND WORRY: This is when you begin to fear the future and worry about what could happen. The real enemy here is not what might happen, it's the fear you are creating. It paralyzes the mind's ability to find creative solutions.

BEING RESENTFUL: If you keep focused on what happened yesterday, you're not available for the good things that might happen today; forgiveness is essential to emotional health.

ANGER: Feel yourself getting angry? Work on getting rid of the anger-and does not mean dumping it on someone else. It means handling it through exercise and humor."

So spend a week outlining what's good about your life, what you're thankful for and work to cut back on gossip, fear. worry and anger. You're guaranteed a good week."

WHAT A GREAT WAY TO CULTIVATE A HAPPY MIND!

Being attractive means many things to many people. A positive attitude assuredly makes us attractive to ALL people. A French philosopher conveys it this way: *"The most manifest sign of wisdom is cheerfulness."*

Some of Leo Buscaglia's wit and wisdom from *"Living, Loving and Learning"* is appropriate here:

"See all criticism as positive, for it leads to self-evaluation. You are always free to reject it, if it is unfair, or if it does not apply to you at all."

"When you get angry, stop and consider all the things you like about them before you respond."

"Don't expect someone else to bring you self-esteem, growth, happiness and fulfillment. You are responsible for those yourself."

"Value yourself. The only people who appreciate a doormat are people with dirty shoes."

"Realize that you always have choices. It's up to YOU!

"Keep laughing. It exercises the heart and protects you from cardiac problems."

And one more little tidbit: "I have dedicated every day of my life to becoming MORE!" How many of us can emulate that? Why not you, today?

Here are four more pertinent quotes, two from ancient and two from modern day philosophers:

"Mix a little foolishness with your serious plans. It's lovely to be silly at the right moment." Horace.

"The supreme happiness of life is the conviction that we are loved." Victor Hugo.

"There is a good side to every situation, and when we find the good side, we automatically whip discouragement and defeat." Dr. Anthony.

And from Robin Leach, host of *"Run Away with the Rich and Famous"*: *"Better a thousand smiles in your heart than a thousand dollars in your pocket."*

For good measure let's add just one more: ***"The ultimate test of whether you possess a sense of humor is your reaction when someone tells you that you don't."*** Frank Tyler.

Since it has been proven in the laboratory that laughter improves the immune system, it logically follows that for ultimate health, we must bring more merriment into our lives.

Resolve to smile automatically, reflecting your confidence in your own well-being, your spouse's health, for any openings, contacts, ideas, or guidance, but most importantly of all, your **gift of life** upon this earth.

Our good friend, Dr. Murphy, advises: **"Let your constant companions be Confidence, Peace, Faith, Love, Joy, Goodwill, Health, Happiness, Inspiration and Abundance."**

To strengthen your new outlook, buy the *"Be Happy Attitudes"* book by the always optimistic and resourceful Rev. Dr. Robert Schuller, author of more than 30 books on demonstrable and rewarding Chrsitianity and the creator of ***Possibility Thinking*** which has transformed countless lives.

Here are some signposts to indicate the road to happiness:

FIRST, make up your mind to be happy. Happiness is often a matter of self-hypnosis. You can think yourself happy just as you can think yourself miserable. Grab all the innocent amusement that comes your way. Never miss an opportunity to have harmless fun. Find pleasure in the simple things."

SECOND, Make the best of your lot. Of course, you don't have everything you want, and things don't always pan out just right for you. Nobody is that lucky.

Even the most fortunate have a few crumpled rose petals under their mattresses. The trick is to find happiness in the lot that has befallen you."

THIRD, Don't take yourself too seriously. Don't think that everything that happens to you is of world-shaking importance and that somehow you should be protected against the misfortunes that befall other people. Don't grow rebellious and morbid over misfortune or sorrow."

FOURTH, Don't take other people too seriously. Don't let their criticisms worry you. You can't please everyone, so please yourself for a change. Don't let your neighbors set standards for you. Be yourself, and try to do the things that YOU enjoy doing, if you want to be comfortable and happy.

FIFTH, Don't borrow trouble. You have to pay compound interest on that and it will bankrupt you. It's a queer thing, but imaginary troubles are harder to bear than real ones. Enjoy today, and let tomorrow take care of itself. And don't forget to smile!"

Albert Schweitzer interposes with; **"You must be prepared to know that life will try to take from you the true and the good when you find it."**

DO NOT LET IT!!!

And finally, learn from the famous Dr. Karl Menninger that *"Attitudes are more important than facts."*

"For a merry heart makes a cheerful countenance." Prov. 15:13.

Let this inspirational sentiment from the Ohio Mason give us the final word:

49

"While you are still young-and all of us are younger today than we shall ever be again-wake up to beauty....it is lavished upon us all, rich or poor, wherever we are-the soul-lifting beauty of a sunrise, a lovely flower, a self-respecting tree, a sun-splashed pathway, a patient river, fluffy clouds luxuriating on a freshly washed sky, a kindly face, the softened shadows nightfall paints, the myriad numbers of stars. The list is endless. Start now to become aware of beauty: let it do its magic. Try each day to make one vivid deposit of beauty in your memory bank. Make sure that you are saving something of intrinsic value for your future besides money.'

WAKE UP TO THIS REALITY

AND

RENEW YOUR LIFE!

PORT VII

SELF – CONFIDENCE

The best book on this subject, and one which I recommend without reservation, is Dr. Anthony's *"The Ultimate Secrets of Total Self-Confidence,"* mentioned in *PORT* 1.

About this characteristic, the author states:

"It goes without saying that to gain self-confidence, we must remove self-doubt. Self-doubt is an acquired condition, and anything acquired can be dropped. Spontaneous self-confidence is there all the time, if we only could but realize it. Your crown of self-confidence is ready for your discovery. Say to yourself, 'I choose to discover my personal strength right now! I need not obey any negative suggestions.' Do not accept your former defeat estimate of your powers. Forget the reasons *why not*-and make a list of the reasons why you can. Declare:

1. **It is my trip.**
2. **I have been bypassing it long enough.**
3. **I, and I only, can make the trip because it is part of me.**

To quote again this popular author who says it so well:

"Creating a positive image of ourselves is CRITICAL. The subconscious works like an automatic pilot. As you change your self-image, you change your subconscious. Our basic self-image was formed when we were about thirteen, and many times influenced by other people's expectations of us. It is all too true that

the price tag the world puts upon us is just about identical to the one we put upon ourselves. **Belief is the thermostat that regulates what we accomplish in life. Therefore the SIZE of our success is determined by the size of our beliefs."**

As we learn to impress the subconscious deeply and regularly, it is well to remember this quote from Dr. Joseph Murphy, D.D.,D.R.S.,PhD.,LL.D. in *"The Power of Your Subconscious Mind":*

"The dominant belief is ALWAYS accepted by the subconscious mind." And Sanaya Roman also reminds us that: **"The less doubt you have about something, the more rapidly it will come. Every belief of a positive nature will return a positive result, and conversely, every negative belief will return a negative result."**

Here's a great jingle to remember:
> **"All things come to him who waits,**
> **But here's a rule that's slicker:**
> **The man who goes for what he wants**
> **Will get it all the quicker."**

In your mind, do you have a problem about being accepted by other people? Again, pretend that you ARE accepted, and you will be. The proof is in the doing.

Ponder that for a moment.

I say without reservation that no greater wisdom can be acquired than to learn the importance of these immortal words: *"For as a man believeth in his heart, so is he."*

Belief is the great motivator. Believe in God, believe in yourself, and believe in the worthwhileness of life.

The great psychologist William James adds: *"In any project, the one important factor is your belief. Without belief, there can be no demonstration."*

In this connection you would find it profitable to read *"The Magic of Believing"* by Claude Bristol. This book will clue you in to the unrealized things that "believing" can make come true for you.

At this time, I want to also strongly recommend that you take some time to read the all-time classic by James Allen: *"As a Man Thinketh"*.

In this book which comes in a miniature hard cover you will find uplifting answers to many of life's troubling questions. It is a great little resource in presenting the guiding principles which enhance circumstances and character. All the books I refer to are books of substance. They are sure to bring about a profound and remarkable change in your life.

What qualities should we seek to instill in ourselves in order to insure our happiness in life?

They are in random order: Cordiality, Diligence, Faith, Generosity, Good Humor, Kindness, Love, Open-mindedness, Patience, Persistence and Resourcefulness.

Queries the perceptive Dr. Anthony: **"Why not believe in your successful destiny? It is just as easy to believe in success as it is to believe in failure. Keep hammering away at the stone of success until you cleave it in two. If you would be strong, build up a dogged faith in yourself-your INNER self. Do not be argued into listlessness by a calendar, a clock, or anybody's idea of how or when things should happen, how long it should take, or who gets the credit.**

I constantly affirm that which I wish, hold it persistently in thought, concentrate all the powers of my mind upon it, and when the mind is sufficiently positive and creative, the desires held-whether it be health, money, or position-will come to me as certainly as a stone that will come to earth when kept far in the air through the attracting influence of gravitation."

Let's follow the above with this affirmation: **"I now make myself a magnet to draw to me the conditions I truly desire."**

As soon as you adopt a confident air, you will be surprised at how soon it will radiate to others, increasing their confidence in your ability.

From Leo Buscaglia, America's great exponent of love, comes this wisdom: **"Maintain your dignity; maintain your integrity. Nobody can put you down except you. They may see you differently, but you know who you are, and you be that something with pride!**

The dynamic and inspiring television pastor of the Crystal Cathedral, Dr. Robert Schuller, reinforces this conviction with what he refers to as the two most important words in his life: "I AM" extending to: ***"I am not free until I believe in me."*** This is the key to the necessary first door you need to open to achieve those worthwhile things in life we all want.

Jesus says in Mark 9:23: ***"If thou canst believe, all things are possible to him that believeth."***

And Ben Sweetland in his two books, *"I Can"* and *"I Will"* states unequivocally: ***"When a person gains a success consciousness, he just will not fail. I have never found a contradictory case."***

William James, one of the greatest authorities on the human mind, emphasizes the same thought this way: *"Believe, and in time, your belief will create the fact."*

The HOW to do it will always come to the person who believes that he CAN do it. Belief is the thermostat that regulates what we accomplish in life. Once you believe in yourself, things DO start happening. Again, Dr. Murphy declares: *"The dominant idea, or belief, is ALWAYS accepted by the subconscious mind."*

To reinforce your drive toward your new personality, write the following directives on five 3x5 cards:

1. **I am building a cheerful, radiant, magnetic and optimistic personality.**
2. **I am using the power of my imagination to build self-confidence and faith in myself and my talents.**
3. **I am using the positive and magnetic drives of my imagination to motivate my life further.**
4. **I am ever conditioning my mind to the eternal qualities of health, happiness and success.**
5. **I maintain a high goal, or dream, for my life for I know that the universe is filled to overflowing with every type of available treasure.**

Rotate these cards often, keeping in mind the directives for that particular day.

Now is a good time to ask yourself: "What kind of qualities do I want to inculcate into my new character?" Go through the alphabet and think of a positive word, or words, which you want to apply to yourself. Preface each attribute with the words, "I AM!" As you go through this process, more and more positive words will suggest themselves to you, giving you the ability to decide which virtues you want to acquire to go with your new image. Repeat these affirmations until you feel they are a natural part of you.

Even after all this input, perhaps you still feel that you have a "what if" consciousness, as I had for many years. If so, just treat this form of negativity in this manner: Just know that if any **"what if"** happens, that you have the capability to handle it. **"What if"** is just another form of self-doubt and you need to banish it from your consciousness.

Always remember that you are a valuable person – *extremely* valuable. You are valuable to God, your Maker, and you are valuable to yourself.

Here are ten great rules to live by from Margery Wilson's *"Double Your Energy and Live Without Fatigue"*:

1. **"Take command of your body, and demand from it a more satisfactory performance every day.**
2. **The force of life is like a powerful presence in which 'we live and move and have our being.'**
3. **I shall assert my God-given right to determine my own condition this day.**
4. **Choose the role you will play.**
5. **Speak in the way that harmonizes with your ideals.**
6. **You must conceive of energy as inexhaustible.**
7. **You must have projects.**
8. **You have at this moment all that you need to remake this stream of consciousness.**
9. **Use everything, but hold the reins yourself.**

10. **Your pattern of claim and acceptance rules your life." Think about *that*.**

And she adds: ***"Since you are a child of the Universe, self-doubt is tantamount to doubt of the Universe and the Great Mind that creates and animates it."***

French moralist La Rochefoucauld has said: ***"The confidence which we have in ourselves gives birth to much of that which we have in others."***

The key to thinking better about yourself is to *pretend* to think better about yourself and you soon will.

Let this be your daily directive

"FAITH IN LIFE, AND LOVE FOR LIFE AND INDIVIDUALS, IS MY WATCHWORD FOR TODAY. SINCE I AM THE MASTER OF MYSELF TODAY, I AM THE MASTER OF EVERY SITUATION. THERE IS WITHIN ME THAT WHICH IS STRONGER THAN ANYTHING OUTSIDE OF ME. EVERY STEP I TAKE THIS DAY IS IN THE DIRECTION OF MORE GOOD – GREATER HAPPINESS. EACH STEP THAT I TAKE AFFORDS ME A GLORIOUS VISION OF MAGNIFICENT ACHIEVEMENT."

HAIL TO THIS DAY!

BELIEVE IN YOUR POTENTIAL

PORT VIII

INSPIRATION and ENTHUSIASM

At this point you may well be asking, "How do I get the necessary drive to carry out the kinds of things you recommend? And how do I become sufficiently inspired and enthusiastic to put more purpose into my life?"

Let's look in the dictionary for the definition of the words *inspiration* and *enthusiasm*.

INSPIRATION: "A divine influence directly and immediately exerted on the mind, or soul, of man."

ENTHUSIASM; "Excited involvement."

When you are inspired, you know that you are no longer a rejected mortal, but a unique part of God's vivacious creation. With "enthusiasm" you feel a wholeness of spirit, bringing to mind the original Greek root of "en" and "theos", meaning in and of God. The sense of the word among the Greeks signified God in us. Inspiration, Enthusiasm, Wholeness – these three go together with a reverence for our Creator.

Emphasizing this euphoric feeling, the Roman poet OVID declares: **"There is a god within us and we *grow* when he stirs us."**

Think back and reflect on how we limit ourselves by not allowing into our imagination things which are outside of accepted logic. Muse on this theme for a moment and decide to set a new and more dynamic path for yoursself.

Say to yourself every morning, "I feel like a MILLION! I look like a million! I am worth a million more!" *Visualize* this feeling as you say it. The visualization is the important thing; otherwise the words are empty expressions and will produce nothing.

Here are more gems to remember:

"A smile always adds to your face value. – Erma Bombeck.

"He who cannot smile should not keep a shop." Chinese proverb.

"Good humor is the health of the soul – sadness is poison." Art Pelozzi.

In the Farmer's Almanac, Vol. 161 is this surprising wisdom: *"I am irresistibly attracting into my experience all the good things my heart desires."*

Say it again, with feeling: *"I am irresistibly attracting into my experience all the good things my heart desires."*

And put some *sparkle* into your speech.

In my own case, I received an awareness of things psychological at an early age when my parents took me to what were then aptly called "psychology lectures." Modern day self-help psychology was just being introduced to the public and all lecturers played to capacity audiences.

Then, just as today, people were hungering for a better and more satisfying way of life and were willing to pay the price, if believable solutions were being offered.

Thus I was grounded early in the field of applied thought.

Dan Custer clearly states in *"Your Miracle of Mind Power"* **"Your mental picture of yourself is not the result – it is the cause. Your Ego-image is the mold out of which your experience emerges."** A principle I did not comprehend for years.

Without realizing it, I was working at odds. I was *pretending* to feel confident on the outside, while on the inside I was not *feeling* what I was affirming on the outside.

In other words, *self-doubt* (that demeaning spectre) was always there lurking in the background.

When someone asks you how you feel? Do you say, "Pretty well, thank you", or some other trite expression? Or do you say, "Fine, thank you" with **gusto?**

Even though you don't feel up to par, the very saying of this simple phrase will not only give you a lift, but will radiate to whomever you meet. Keep this quality forever a part of your personality, for the wholeheartedness and enthusiasm of your reply, not only does you good; It becomes a tonic to your friends.

Optimists say, *"Enthusiasm makes things 110% better!"* Even if you don't agree with this percentage, the plus value is always there. In everything you do, live it up!

When asked about the secret of his success, Mark Twain told his listeners: *"I was born excited."* Enthusiasm is an excellent lubricant for the mind.

Get excited about life – the wonder of life! *Excitement, enthusiasm, inspiration*: Drink this tonic often. Always broadcast good news – not misfortune.

Ella Wheeler Wilcox, 19th century American poet and journalist, puts it poetically thus:

"TALK HEALTH! THIS DREARY, NEVER-CHANGING TALE
OF MORTAL MALADIES IS WORN AND STALE.
YOU CANNOT CHARM, OR INTEREST, OR PLEASE

BY HARPING ON THAT MINOR CHORD DISEASE.
SAY YOU ARE WELL, OR ALL IS WELL WITH YOU;

AND GOD SHALL HEAR YOUR WORDS AND
MAKE THEM TRUE."

Whatever your disposition, it is believing that there *is* a solution that is of paramount importance. Emerson impels us to: **"Assume in your imagination as *already yours* the goal you aspire to have. Enter into the part ENTHUSIASTICALLY!"** and again, he warns that: **"Nothing great was ever achieved without *enthusiasm.*"**

A giant in the automotive industry, a pioneer in mass production and the living wage, as well as the inventor of the common man's motor car, Henry Ford reinforces the need for that vital essence with this wisdom: **"You can do anything if you have enthusiasm. Enthusiasm is the yeast that makes your hopes rise to the stars. Enthusiasm is the sparkle in your eyes, the swing in your gait, the grip of your hand, the irresistible surge of will and energy to execute your ideas. Enthusiasts are fighters. They have fortitude. They have staying qualities. Enthusiasm is at the bottom of all progress. With it there is accomplishment. Without it, there are only alibis."**

I am sure you are beginning to see that inspiration and enthusiasm are inseparable. When you are enthusiastic, you are inspired and when you are truly inspired, you know that you are not a rejected mortal, but a unique factor in God's ever-evolving creation!

KathrynKullman, the great religious lecturer and healer often declared: ***"I believe in miracles because I believe in God."***

Unbelievable as it may seem to the sophisticated mind, miracles are happening every day. We have to look beneath the surface to see and to sense them.

"Remember that a miracle cannot prove that which is impossible. It is a confirmation of that which is possible."
–Dr. Joseph Murphy

French novelist Honoré de Balzac was right when he said, *"Miracles are within us – natural facts which some call supernatural."*

And author Bovee observes: *"We trifle when we assign limits to our desires, since Nature has set none."*

The achievement of a heart-felt desire will in itself seem like a miracle. Actually, every cubic inch of space and every hour of light and dark are miracles of their own kind. Universal skepticism of miracles is understandable. It takes a childlike faith to believe in the seemingly impossible.

William Arthur Ward gives us seven simple ways to begin living a more abundant, exciting, productive and rewarding life, viz:

1. **MEMORIZE at least one great truth every day. It may be an inspiring poem, an especially helpful verse of Scripture, an affirmation, or a favorite quotation. What you memorize becomes a part of your life, your character and your future.**
2. **CRYSTALLIZE your goals, your aspirations and your ambitions. Write them down and include a workable timetable for their accomplishment.**
3. **SPECIALIZE in some particular field of endeavor. Become an expert, and you will soon**

become **indispensable.** Become an authority, and you will inevitably become sought after.

4. NEUTRALIZE your fears, your doubts and your anxieties through the power of prayer, meditation and a positive attitude.

5. MINIMIZE your shortcomings, your liabilities and your seeming deficiencies. Because you were designed by a Master Architect, you are greater than you think.

6. MAXIMIZE your abilities, your talents, your potentialities and your possibilities. Accentuate your positives!

7. RECOGNIZE the good in others, the beauty of friendships, the splendor of love, and the joy of service. Train your eyes to look for the best in others, and invariably others will see the best in you.

The Rev. Robert H. Schuller, world-famous television pastor of the Crystal Cathedral in Garden Grove, California, tells us to challenge ourselves with this question: *"What great thing would I attempt, if I knew I could not fail?"*

To inspire us to soul-satisfying achievement, the poet Goethe directs us: *"To dare to dream what we dare to do."*

And now imbibe this enlightening and genuine definition of Greatness:

GREATNESS

"A man is as great as the dreams he dreams,
As great as the love he bears,
As great as the values he redeems,
As the happiness he shares.
A man is as great as the thoughts he thinks,
As the worth he has attained;
As the fountain at which his spirit drinks,
As the insight he has gained.
A man is as great as the truth he speaks,
As the kind of help he gives,
As great as the destiny he seeks,
As great as the life he lives."

DREAM AND DARE TO DO!

To further bring God's miracles into your own life, pray *"The Prayer of Jabez"*, from the book of the same name by Dr. Bruce Wilkinson. Get this book, which has become a best seller (having already sold some 7,000,000 copies), and see for yourself the astonishing happenings Dr. Wilkinson has experienced by using this prayer.

M. Frazier Keables

PORT IX

ENERGY, POWER and PROSPERITY

Are you enjoying the journey thus far? Are you beginning to feel a newness of spirit? Are you sensing a vivacity of life you did not know before? As you ingest the authentic principles we are reading about, you *will* begin to *glow* inside. It is inevitable, so pause and absorb the wisdom thus far.

When we feel our best, we sense a boundless capability. How do we develop and awaken this inherent potential buried deep within our psyche?

Let's start with a quotation from Isaiah with which you may be familiar. Margery Wilson paraphrases it in this fashion: **"But they that wait upon the Lord (the law, or how things rightfully should go) shall renew their strength; they shall mount up with wings as eagles; they shall run and not grow weary; they shall walk and not faint."**

And she continues: **"Make this resolution now: Never again will I speak in defeat, or limitations, with suspicion, or for spite, or timidly. Avoid all words that you don't want to be translated into your life as personal experiences. The secret is in the power of the inner mind.**

"Turn from the 'law' of diminishing returns to the LAW of accruing force. It is childiish, immature, ignorant, blind and animalistic to live and think in terms of punishing limits. Accept them now, if you must, but send your mind ahead of your steps into the blessed freedom of the strength, beauty and riches of

the world in which you 'live, move and have your being.'

Your life will begin to change. Your body will begin to change. You shall see God in your flesh. For life and energy are mind. All change, all creation begins with concept. Your concept is your pattern for your tomorrows. Put the world of mind before the world of material. One or the other will be the master in our lives. One is expanding and the other limiting. By treating the 'material' as the servant of the mind, we elevate it and multiply its use."

And Charlotte P. Gilman concurs with: **"A concept is even stronger than a fact."**

In *Personal Power Through Awareness*, Sanaya Roman adds this: **"There are many ways to bring up your energy. Start by being aware of what you say to people. Are you building them up? Are you holding an ennobling vision of them? Whatever you point a finger at, will grow. If you have any situation in your life that is not working, the more you picture it as not working, the more you create it so.**

You can change the energy between yourself and anyone else by using positive words.

If you can change even some of the thousands of thoughts which flow through your mind every day with thoughts of joy, health and abundance, you will rapidly change what you experience."

Pause and drink in the above. Repeat it to yourself and sense its impact. You can never be better than your own self-esteem, and the above is a way to raise it.

"When we realize the truth of our own Being, we become aware that we are the individualization of the infinite Life, and that the Divine Consciousness in us is

the *only* power. **By our own consciousness, we realize the awareness of the Divine Principle and by doing so, it releases the Divine Energy through our being, eliminating all untoward conditions.**" So says Murdo Macdonald-Bayne 'Eliminating all untoward conditions?' Now that's a tall order. But, let's pursue this approach to see where it will lead us.

We should remember **"For man shall not live by bread alone, but by every word that proceedeth out of the mouth of God."** Mat:4:4

Dr. Murphy enlarges on this concept with this reflection: **"Realize and know that God is all Bliss, Joy, Indescribable Beauty, Absolute Harmony, Infinite Intelligence and Boundless Love; and that He is Omnipotent, Supreme, and the only Presence. Mentally accept that God is all these things as unhesitatingly as you accept the fact that you are alive. Then you will begin to experience in your life the wonderful results of your new conviction about the Blessed God within you. You will find your health, your vitality, your business, your environment and the world in general all changing for the better. You will begin to prosper spiritually, mentally and materially. Your understanding and spiritual insight will grow in a wonderful way, and you will find yourself transformed into a new man."**

"Be ye therefore transformed by the *renewing* of your mind that ye may prove what is that good and acceptable and perfect will of God." Rom:12:2. Here we see the Biblical corollary of the previous quotes.

Let us now recognize that the source of all energy is that inexhaustible creative Power we call God (originally Yahweh). If you can begin to feel that you are in touch with this awesome Power, you will sense a surge of energy.

And why not? Since this energy is all around us, we have the latent ability to tap into this all-encompassing source at any time.

My introspective mother used to say: "Use the affirmation, **'I am filled with Power!'**" And why not, if God is within and without all things? She used to add: **"Nothing can stop a powerful man – a man filled with the illimitable power of the Universe."**

We are all filled with electricity. To prove this, all we have to do is scuff on a rug, or be out in the cold weather and touch a piece of metal. Zap! The static electricity will snap, and you will instantaneously feel the miniature shock.

Here, then, let us ask ourselves a momentous question: Can we connect our own electricity to the energy of the Universe?

Powerful thought, this!

Richard S. Clarke in his book, *"You Have One Life-Give it Your Best Shot"* emphasizes this connection, viz: **"Once you realize that your own mind has a direct wire to the Universal Mind and learn how to let that Universal Mind know what your need is, there will be no lack or limitation in your own life. When you comprehend that your own mind is connected to the Universal, or God-Mind, you will have taken your first step toward creating the kind of environment you really want, toward rising above your present circumstances."** The powerful impact of this awareness will completely enlarge your horizons.

We are reminded of this all-encompassing electrical energy by the lightning in a thunderstorm. At most other times we are not aware of it.

Margery Wilson claims **that *"Energy is a principle you can touch."*** Read her book, *"Double Your Energy and*

Live Without Fatigue". It is a treasure house of recommendations about how to get more out of life and how to extend your own energy level.

When by your own enlightenment you begin to experience this linkage, you will then come to sense the constant dynamic inflow of energy to you from the Fountainhead of all power- the Supreme and Sole Creator of the Universe.

The above author again advises us: **"When you want more light from a lamp, you simply exchange the smaller electric bulb for a larger one, thus making a larger claim on the great supply back of it. Do the same with your energy."**

Now do you begin to see how you can recharge your own energy by connecting with the Master Power Station?

Probably not, but consider its phenomenal significance!

Let's explore the possibilities together. How can we go about lighting this light within us so that we can radiate its glow to others?

Sanaya Roman answers it this way: **"By filling ourselves with light and love-the warm glow you feel when you are euphoric. By doing this, you will find that this light and love will constantly regenerate itself and be an attraction to others."**

The minute we were born we possessed a unique radiance, seen perhaps, only by our mothers. This light *"which lighteth every man who comes into this world"* is always with us. Until we recognize this indwelling divinity, we cannot experience it, or even sense its presence. To become aware of this marvel, we must become ready to learn "as a little child."

Prov.4:20-22 counsels us to: **"Pay attention, my child, to what I say. Listen carefully. Don't lose sight of my**

words. Let them penetrate deep within your heart, for they bring life and *radiant* health to anyone who discovers their meaning."

In *"You Try It"* Robert A. Russell puts it succinctly thus: *"The light of God is to your soul what the rays of the sun are to the germ in the planted bulb. It is the life of your Being."*

Catch this illuminating concept, which is broadly expressed in Psalm 36:9; *"For with Thee is the Fountain of Life; in Thy Light shall we see light."*

A fountain of Life? Can you picture such a fountain and see the water shooting up in many directions; and can you visualize a powerful light shining on this effervescence picking up the myriad colors?

This is what your life can be: Emitting **brilliance** to all you meet, and your character imbued with many hues – if you once realize that *YOU* are a supremely important droplet to this Fountain of Life!

Isn't this Utopian vision worth your vigilant attention?

It is St. Paul who informs us in II Cor. 5:17: **"If any man be in Christ, he is a new creation; old things are passed away; behold, all things are become new."** And they become '*new*' by the '*renewing of our mind*.' Rom. 12:2.

Do you feel that you need more energy to cope with the special problems which confront you? Think about Margery Wilson's advice: **"Energy flows in when inferiority flows out."** Simple and demonstrable.

Sanaya Roman adds: **"There are currents of energy that circle the planet and you can tap into them anytime you want. If you want physical energy, you can breathe deeply and imagine that you are connected to the flow of all the people who have an abundance of vitality."**

Tune into their flow of high, successful energy. Through your breathing, you can draw in your global connection onto other people, or to the assistance and guidance from the higher forces of the Universe."

Alexis Carrel, late Fellow of the American College of Surgeons, Nobel prize winner, and famed Rockefeller University biochemist, makes this revealing statement: "Prayer, like radium, is a luminous and self-generating form of energy."

In the following treatise, (which I am including verbatim) he enlarges on this perceptive concept:

(Read on and you will find your faith in prayer renewed

"Prayer is not only worship; it is also an invisible emanation of man's worshipping spirit – the most powerful form of energy that one can generate. The influence of prayer on the human mind and body is as demonstrable as that of secreting glands. Its results can be measured in terms of increased physical buoyancy, greater intellectual vigor, moral stamina, and a deeper understanding of the realities underlying human relationships.

If you make a habit of sincere prayer, your life will be very noticeably and profoundly altered. Prayer stamps with its indelible mark our actions and demeanor. A tranquility of bearing, a facial and bodily response, are observed in those whose inner lives are thus enriched. Within the depths of consciousness a flame kindles. And man sees himself. He discovers his selfishness, his silly pride, his fears, his greeds, his blunders. He develops a sense of moral obligation, intellectual humility. Thus begins a journey of the soul toward the realm of grace.

TAPS THE SOURCE OF ENERGY

Prayer is a force as real as terrestrial gravity. As a physician, I have seen men, after all other therapy had failed, lifted out of disease and melancholy by the serene effort of prayer. It is the only power in the world that seems to overcome the so-called 'laws of nature'; the occasions on which prayer has done this have been termed 'miracles.' But a constant, quieter miracle takes place hourly in the hearts of men and women who have discovered that prayer supplies them with a steady flow of sustaining power in their daily lives.

NOT EMPTY FORM

Too many people regard prayer as a formalized routine of words, a refuge for weaklings, or a childish petition for material things. We sadly undervalue prayer when we conceive of it in these terms, just as we should underestimate rain by describing it as something that fills the birdbath in our garden. Properly understood, prayer is a mature activity indispensable to the fullest development of personality – the ultimate integration of man's highest faculties. Only in prayer do we achieve that complete and harmonious assembly of body, mind and spirit which gives the frail human reed its unshakable strength.

The words 'Ask and it shall be given you' have been verified by the experience of humanity. True, prayer may not restore the dead child to life, or bring relief from pain. But prayer, like radium, is a source of luminous, self-generating energy.

IN TUNE WITH THE INFINITE

How does prayer fortify us with so much dynamic power?

To answer this question (admittedly outside the jurisdiction of science), I must point out that all prayers have one thing in common. The triumphant hosannas of a great oratorio, or the humble supplications of an Iriquois hunter begging for luck in the chase, demonstrate the same truth; that humans seek to augment their finite energy by addressing themselves to the infinite source of all energy. When we pray, we link ourselves with the inexhaustible motive power that spins the universe. We ask that a portion of this power be apportioned to our needs. Even in asking, our human deficiencies are filled and we arise strengthened and repaired.

But we must never summon God merely for the gratification of our whims. We derive most power from prayer, not as a petition, but as a supplication that we may be more like Him. Prayer should be regarded as a practice of the Presence of God.

An old peasant was seated alone in the last pew of the village church. 'What are you waiting for?' he was asked, and he answered, 'I am looking at Him and He is looking at me.' Man prays not only that God should remember him, but also that he should remember God.

PRAYER WORKS A CHANGE IN US

How can prayer be defined? Prayer is the effort of man to reach God, to commune with an invisible Being, Creator of all things, supreme wisdom, truth, beauty and strength, Father and Redeemer of each man. The goal of prayer always remains hidden to intelligence. For both language and thought fail when we attempt to describe God.

We do know, however, that whenever we address God in fervent prayer, we change both soul and body for the better. It could not happen that any man or woman could pray for a single moment without some good result. 'No man ever prayed,' said Emerson, 'without learning something.'

One can pray everywhere, in the streets, the office, the shop, the school, as well as in the solitude of one's own room, or among the crowd in a church. There is no prescribed posture, time or place.

TRUE PRAYER A WAY OF LIFE

'Think of God more often than you breathe,' said Epictetus, the Stoic. In order to really modify your personality, prayer must become a habit. It is meaningless to pray in the morning and live like a barbarian the rest of the day. True prayer is a way of life; the truest life is literally a way of prayer.

The best prayers are like improvisations of gifted lovers, always about the same thing, yet never twice the same. We cannot all be as creative in prayer as St. Theresa or Bernard of Clairvaux, both of whom poured their adoration into words of mystical beauty. Fortunately, we do not need eloquence – our slightest impulse to prayer is recognized by God. Even if we are pitifully dumb, or if our tongues are overlaid with vanity or deceit, our meager syllables of praise are acceptable to Him, and He showers us with strengthening manifestations of His love.

PRELUDE TO A BETTER WORLD

Today, as never before, prayer is a binding necessity in the lives of men and nations. The lack of emphasis on the religious sense has brought the world to the edge of destruction. Our deepest source of power and perfection has been left miserably underdeveloped.

Prayer, the basic exercise of the spirit, must be actively practiced in our private lives. The neglected soul of man must be made strong enough to assert itself once more. For if the power of prayer is again released and used in the lives of common men and women, if the spirit declares its aims clearly and boldly, there is yet hope that our prayers for a better world will be answered."

Dr. Carrel had long been impressed by the fact that many of life's phenomena could not be scientifically explained. He knew, for example, that miracles of healing are possible; he spent weeks at Lourdes studying them, and never forgot the day he saw a cancerous sore shrivel to a scar before his eyes. Dr. Carrel concluded thirty three years of brilliant research at the Rockefeller Institute in 1939. Among his many honors were the Nordhoff-Jung model for cancer research and the Nobel prize for success in suturing blood vessels.

Here, then, is compelling proof that *prayer* is **YOUR** connection to the all-encompassing energy of the Universe!

How, then, should we pray?

1. **You must be devout. In a spirit of thankfulness, you must pray with your whole heart (your whole being).**
2. **You must believe. You must have faith that your prayer will be answered.**
3. **You must envision. You must visualize the beneficial outcome.**

As the Bible says: **"Be careful for nothing, but in everything by prayer and supplication with**

***thanksgiving* let your requests be made known to God."**
Phil.4:6.

Now for some valuable thoughts on prosperity:

A good place for us to start is in Proverbs where we read: **"By humility and the fear of (respect for) the Lord (the understanding of the law) are riches and honor and life."**

Let's continue with Vernon Howard's viewpoint: **"The realization of my natural mental health brings an awareness of impending financial success."**

Dr. Anthony confirms this with the following: **"Your mental attitudes toward your money-making abilities have everything to do with your financial condition. When you believe there is a Way, you automatically convert negative energy into positive energy."**

Bob Conklin in his *"The Dynamics of Successful Attitudes"* gives us this recipe for financial freedom:

1. **Maintain your desire to be free from debt.**
2. **Bless each debt and the person owed**
3. **Ask God to prosper them and to prosper you.**
4. **Ask for the right way to pay your creditors.**
5. **Start paying some small debt, as you can, on your way to freedom from all debts.**
6. **No matter what station you are in life, thank God for it. A spirit of thankfulness does wonders for any personality.**

And "Write down the things you want from life and ***EXPECT THEM TO COME TRUE.***"

Let us always remember that God does supply us with infinite resources to meet our every need, and that each new minute is rich with promise.

II Chron 20:20 tells us: ***"Believe in the Lord your God so shall ye be established; believe His prophets, so shall ye prosper."***

In *"Universal Science"* Frank Picard states: **"If you can succeed in analyzing your circumstances without using the word 'but' you will be astounded at what will happen to your finances."**

And Dr. Scott Gerson advises: **"Do not make competition 'copytition.' Put purpose first and you are headed toward riches."** These are the *riches* of an enlightened consciousness.

Again Bob Conklin adds this: **"There is only one way you can save money, and that is to treat savings as an expense. If you pay all of your other bills first and hope there is some left for savings, there never will be. Security is a feeling. Saving money is the action that helps create that feeling."**

Now to carry this approach a little further, Dr. Gerald Mann (1-877-353-HOPE) recommends that out of your earnings you give 10% to God, 10% to savings *before* you use the rest. Try it.

A simple affirmation to say is:

"I'm successful – I can do

All my spirit wants me to.

I now am rich; I now am strong;

Healthy, Wealthy, all day long."

Dr. Murphy likes to think of supply in this way: ***"My Good is now flowing to me freely, joyously, unendingly."***

"**They that seek the Lord shall not want any good thing.**" (Psalms 34:10). Let us see if we can demonstrate this promise in our own lives, not sometime in the future, but NOW!

Jesus Christ has said, *"I am come that they might have life and have it more ABUNDANTLY."* (John 10:10) Do we need more proof than this that Abundance, Happiness, Success and Fulfillment are what God wants for all of us?

We are reminded of this so many times in both the Old and the New Testaments. Isn't it time we believed it? Emphatically, it is time that we accepted this Truth and began to demonstrate it in our lives Here and Now!

Ralph Waldo Emerson gives us this definition of True Success: "**To laugh often and much; to win the respect of intelligent people and the affection of children; to earn the appreciation of honest critics and endure the betrayal of false friends; to appreciate beauty; to find the best in others; to leave the world a bit better, whether by a healthy child, a garden patch, or a redeemed social condition; to know even one life has breathed easier because you lived. This is to have succeeded.**"

DRINK IN THE ENERGIZING FRESHNESS OF EACH NEW DAY!

"IF YOU WISH THE WORLD WERE BETTER,
LET ME TELL YOU WHAT TO DO;
SET A WATCH UPON YOUR ACTIONS;
KEEP THEM ALWAYS STRAIGHT AND TRUE.
RID YOUR MIND OF SELFISH MOTIVES,
LET YOUR THOUGHTS BE PURE AND HIGH;
YOU CAN MAKE A LITTLE EDEN
OF THE SPHERE YOU OCCUPY."

And YOU can do it!

THROUGH GUIDANCE and GROWTH

M. Frazier Keables

PORT X

ESSENTIAL TRUTHS AND AFFIRMATIONS

"He who knows, and knows he knows, is wise; follow him. He who knows, and knows not he knows, is asleep; wake him. He who knows not, and knows not he knows not, is a fool; shun him. He who knows not, and knows he knows not, is a child; teach him." Arabian proverb.

It may take some discernment to comprehend this classic epigram, but think it through and find the great wisdom expressed here.

Only YOU have the power to change, to redirect your thinking. Start by following St. Paul's advice: **"Finally, brethren, whatsoever things are true, whatsoever things are honest, whatsoever things are just, whatsoever things are pure, whatsoever things are lovely, whatsoever things are of good report; if there be any virtue, if there be any praise, think on these things."** Phil. 4:8

And in proportion as you fill your mind with *'these things'* will you bring these virtues into your own life.

Here is the speech given by General Douglas MacArthur to a group of plebes from West Point who were visiting him the day before he died:

"People grow old only by deserting their ideals; years may wrinkle their skin, but to give up their interests wrinkles their soul. You are as young as your self-confidence, as old as your fears, as young as your hope, as old as your despair. In the central place of every heart is a

83

sounding chamber. As long as it receives messages of faith, hope and courage, so long does it remain young.

When your heart is full of the snows of pessimism, and the ice of cynicism, then and only then, have you grown old, and as the ballard says, 'you just fade away'."

That is the way he wanted people to perceive his demise: this giant of a man who had experienced two World Wars and was not only the chief architect in achieving the peace, but also in bringing renewal to Japan.

So be guided by these ideals and infuse your mind with the affirmations of the things you have set your heart on. In fact, view these goals as *already* accomplished. Keep the awareness that God wants you to be fulfilled and remember *visualization* is the key.

As Roy Eugene Davis observes: *"Your dominating thoughts mold your consciousness, and your state of consciousness determines your lot in life."* (A truth not generally perceived, but one which needs to be repeated over and over).

All right then, let's hear that again, *'dominating thoughts'*....have we ever thought about just what our 'dominating thoughts' are? Take time now to contemplate just what constitutes *your* dominating thoughts. If they determine our lot in life, then it is imperative that we analyze them and decide from here on in to make those thoughts beneficial to our heartfelt desires in life.

As we expand our outlook, let's look for these new dimensions:

"A strange excitement taps my heart,
For suddenly I am a part
Of life that smiles and life that grieves
Somehow I'm one with all that breathes
I know I'm in a new dimension,
Yet it demands my close attention.
The door of life is now ajar;
I start to see things as they are.
All the phenomena I see
Are really taking place in me;
And all at once I am aware
Of life within and not out there.
Now everywhere I chance to look
Brings memories of life's great book.
One line I especially recall:
God's kingdom is within us all!!!"

By Marilyn Louks

And the 19th century poet, Robert Browning puts it beautifully this way:

"Truth is within ourselves....
There is an inmost center in us all,
Where Truth abides in fullness...and to know,
Rather consists in opening out a way
Whence the imprisoned splendor may escape."

At this time you may still be wondering, "What is this truth I am seeking? Does it not stand to reason that what we are intuitively seeking is the comprehension of our True Self, or the Truth of Being?

As the eminent German theologian, Dr. Paul Tillich, points out: **"For in the depth of every serious doubt and every despair of truth, the passion for truth is still at work. Don't give in too quickly to those who want to alleviate your anxiety about truth. Don't be seduced into a truth which is not really *your* truth."**

You will find your understanding further amplified by Dr. Kenneth Walker, author of *"The Extra Sensory Mind."* **"It is at this moment of inner quietness, of newly revealed freedom, of heightened being, that something of a much more real nature makes its presence felt. Perhaps we have been seeking truth all our lives, or else asking to be led to it by some teacher whom we believe to know more than we do, but we have never succeeded in finding what we sought.**

And now, at this quiet moment, because we are ready for truth, and have transcended that which had hitherfore stood·between the truth and us – truth comes to us uninvited, conferring on us also happiness with its magic touch."

"Happiness with its magic touch"-that ecstatic state so sought after by the whole world.

The question remains: Is such a rapturous state achievable? When we trust wholeheartedly in the goodness of life, we will then find the timing of things to be coming into sync with our innermost feelings and to begin to sense that elusive harmony.

When a negative thought does come to mind, replace it with a SUNSHINE thought. Your improved state of mind will soon result in a more balanced outlook. As you do this, you will be giving your life a new and more decisive meaning.

NOW is always the time to initiate a new direction. Remember you always respond to the way you look and a happy look is indispensable.

The famous Chinese author and philology authority Lin Yutang adds this: ***"It is not so much what you believe that matters, as the way in which you believe it, and translate that belief into action."***

In other words, what I do today determines the kind of life I will have tomorrow.

My own little doggerel is this:

> ***"Let sorrow be incidental,***
> ***Let joy be monumental;***

Resolve: ***My words will ever cheer***
> ***Each individual here.***
> ***Youth, vitality being expressed;***
> ***Staying in tune will do the rest."***

(IT TAKES BOTH RAIN AND SUNSHINE TO MAKE A RAINBOW)

In the *"The Power of Positive Thinking"* Norman Vincent Peale asks us to remember that *"An inflow of new thoughts can remake you regardless of every difficulty you may now face, and I repeat, every difficulty."*

"And from the Sanskrit comes this enlightening interpretation of the phrase "to pray": To judge yourself wonderfully made."

M. Frazier Keables

"IF THERE IS RIGHTEOUSNESS IN THE HEART
THERE WILL BE BEAUTY IN THE CHARACTER,
IF THERE IS BEAUTY IN THE CHARACTER
THERE WILL BE HARMONY IN THE HOME.
IF THERE IS HARMONY IN THE HOME,
THERE WILL BE ORDER IN THE NATION,
WHEN THERE IS ORDER IN THE NATION,
THERE WILL BE PEACE IN THE WORLD."
CHINESE PROVERB

THUS BE UPLIFTED & INSPIRED!

PORT XI

VISUALIZATION AND REALIZATION

First, the WORD – the mental image. This is the mold.

Second, the FLUX. Throw your spirit around as much of the appropriated energy as you need to fill your mold.

You have only to BELIEVE-to KNOW-you have it, in order to give that flux time to harden (to evolve); so that all may see it, and for you to see your dreams come true.

There it is in a nutshell, but we need to broaden this concept to clarify what is meant by the above formula.

"When you visualize and keep the pictures CONSTANT, action follows, because action, after all, is nothing more than Energized Thought. Whatever your mind can conceive, believe, and picture, MUST become a reality for you." –Dr. Anthony

And Sanaya Roman adds: **"The less doubt you have about getting something, the more rapidly it will come. Acting upon intuition requires flexibility and spontaneity as well as faith."**

So true!

Again, this helpful note from the same author: **"If you are forcing yourself to do one thing while your feelings are urging you to do something else, you are not paying attention to your intuition."**

So let's begin to listen to these silent urgings which do not always coincide with practical reason. If we don't ask why and just press ahead, we will begin to sense the promptings of our inner feelings to steer us in a more favorable direction.

Dr. Anthony proclaims: **"The Law of Magnetic Attraction can bring you that which you picture in detail. Visualize your wishes as clearly as possible; not only see them, but *FEEL* them. They are already a reality, once they have been visualized, for that is the law of Mind."**

For, as Margery Wilson concludes: *"Your concept is your pattern for your tomorrows."* This is the all-important formula in a nutshell.

Here are even more elucidating words from William James, one of the most distinguished scholars, eminent philosophers, and early pioneers of modern day psychology: *"The greatest discovery of our age is that man, by changing the inner aspects of his thinking, can change the outer aspects of his life."*

Here you begin to see how the law of mental magnetism works to attract our true wants.

In *"Riches Within Your Reach,"* Robert Collier puts it this way: **"If you will put the God within you into some worthwhile endeavor, and *believe* in Him, you can overcome any poverty, any handicap, any untoward circumstances."** (A reiteration of Page 49).

I am sure that for most of us that is stretching our imagination to limits we cannot comprehend. Where and what is this God within us? Put simply, it is our True Individuality coming to light. If we will look within and seek out this Divine Endowment, call on It, and put It to work in solving our problems and achieving our goals, then we will be able to say with Robert Collier that the negatives in our lives can be, and will be overcome.

Let's get to work on it right now and start to prove that *"with God all things are possible."* With inspiration, faith and understanding, we can accomplish far more than we had ever hoped for and can actually *renew* our life.

Count on it!

Don't just read this book. Picture the goals you are seeking, get involved in attaining them and expand your horizons.

Are there solutions we haven't yet discovered?

Heed these reassurances from the Master Teacher:

"I say unto you, ask and it shall be given you; seek and you shall find; knock and it shall be opened unto you."

"Therefore, I say unto you, Whatsoever things you desire when you pray, BELIEVE that you receive them and you shall have them."

(And relax about the eventual manifestation).

Sanaya Roman infuses this concept: **"Imagine! 40,000 to 50,000 thoughts go through your mind every day. If you can turn even 2,000 of them into thoughts of light, love, abundance, and joy, you will quickly change what you experience in life."**

Let us then stimulate this subconscious mind by our own creative images, by noble thoughts, and by intense desires. All theological thinkers agree that we have this power within us, although they may call it by different names. The power to visualize; the power to create; the power to overcome; such is our awesome power from God!

Here's something else to think about: **"Fix firmly upon anything, good or bad, in the world, and you attract it to you, or are attracted to it in obedience to the Law. You attract to you the things you expect, think about, and hold in your mental attitude. This is no**

superstitious idea, but a firmly established, scientific, psychological fact." –Robert Collier.

Perceiving that the 'Kingdom of God' is within us, we now know that we have the innate ability to accomplish far more than we formerly thought possible, and that our goals are *not* unreachable.

Now we begin to ask ourselves, what does this realization embrace? It means that all of God's values and attributes such as love, strength, peace, harmony, happiness and abundance must be, and are, within us to the degree that we can perceive them and can be activated by our comprehension of God's creative Spirit.

"For God created man in His own image, in the image of God He created him; male and female, He created them." Gen. 1:27

If you can realize even for an instant that you inherently possess these qualities even in infinitesimal measure, you will soon manifest the evidence of this illumination in your outward appearance and within your body.

Vernon Howard gives us these excellent guidelines in "**Word Power:**"

1. **Fascination with my own mental make-up is the clue to broader understanding.**
2. **Going forward as a personal adventure in my own best way carries rich rewards.**
3. **My daily thoughts can produce profitable transformation both within and without.**
4. **As my ability grows to increasingly command circumstances, other conditions come more and more under my control.**
5. **An awareness of my limitless thought power will provide a much richer life for me.**

6. I am now aware that I have the inherent ability to choose positive and constructive thoughts and actions.
7. The all-powerful guidance of intuition and right motives are an inspiration to greater achievement.
8. As my freedom from negativity grows, so will my spontaneity.
9. The excitement of finding out the great truths about self are a stimulus to my entire Being.
10. I am finding that the faculty of 'understanding' is the great treasure referred to in the Bible and has become my guide to a happier life.

As we realize more of our own potential through the divinity within us, the law of magnetic attraction begins to work, inspiring us *anew*.

Therefore, *'Choose this day whom ye shall serve,'* holding in mind those positive qualities which will bring their own rich reward. For this Universal Kingdom of God is within each one of us, could we but realize it.

Dr. Murphy encourages us: **"To smile automatically, reflecting your happiness and gratefulness for your present state of health, for your spouse's health, for any openings, contacts, ideas, guidance, and more importantly, for your gift of life on this earth. Let your constant companions be Confidence, Peace, Faith, Love, Joy, Goodwill, Health, Happiness, Guidance, Inspiration and Abundance."**

Being in tune with the cosmic forces of the Universe is as essential to recognizing the eternality of life as is skepticism of high principles the most destructive form of ignorance.

In Norman Vincent Peale's *"The Power of Positive Thinking"* is this interpretation of the Bible passage: **"In Him we live (that is, have vitality), and move (have dynamic energy), and have our Being (attain completeness), bringing once more to light a realization of our true nature."**

Again, let us read from Margery Wilson's treatise: **"The force of life is....like a powerful presence in which we 'live and move and have our being.' The life-force is always working for you. It is always building, healing, protecting, re-using the material at hand in a miraculous fashion. All it needs is a chance. Therefore, choose the fine, truly, kindly, rich, sympathetic, encouraging, and vigorous words that go with your new 'part.' This person would spend no time talking about sickness, failure, or disaster of any kind of evil, if he or she could help it. (If anybody thinks this mode of procedure is too sweet for words, just try it). You will discover that it takes all of your strength, discipline, courage and self-control to make it."**

Are you still holding onto a dream which has been a vital part of you for an indefinite time? (I can relate to that). All of us have these secret dreams hidden away inside of us which we don't reveal to anyone. Is it a dream which you still believe in, but somehow it seems unattainable?

Then do as Basil King advises: "Be **bold** and mighty forces will come to your aid."

Pursue and believe in this dream and in its realization. Through guidance from God and from the enlightenment you are discovering in this book, you are putting yourself on the path of a favorable outcome.

Langston Hughes tells us to:

"HOLD FAST TO DREAMS, FOR IF DREAMS DIE,
LIFE IS A BROKEN-WINGED BIRD THAT
CANNOT FLY."

And from Samuel Longfellow:

"THE FREER STEP, THE FULLER BREATH,
THE WIDE HORIZON'S GRANDER VIEW;
THE SENSE OF LIFE THAT KNOWS NO DEATH;
THE LIFE THAT MAKETH ALL THINGS NEW."

What a Utopian, yet practical concept!
It's forever yours to indulge in NOW!

AS YOUR CONCEPTS ARE RENEWED.

M. Frazier Keables

PORT XII

THE SUPERCONSCIOUS, THE CONSCIOUS and THE SUBCONSICOUS MINDS

I think that we can all agree that such a designation as the Superconscious Mind would have to be the all-knowing, ever-guiding, all-powerful, and ever-present Source of our Being – our Creator! *"For in Him we live, and move, and have our being,"* though how little we are conscious of this connection.

We are all well aware of our conscious mind, since we live with it every day of our lives, and are cognizant of its presence every waking moment.   In contrast, the subconscious mind seems to be an unknown and unrealized force, but let's think of it as our link between the conscious and the Superconscious Mind. We are well aware that we can use the conscious mind to benefit, or destroy, us. So, let's learn to use the subconscious to connect us to the "good life."

Now we need to find that inner guidance which comes when we are in tune with all three.

Did you ever think that *"The result in one's life is determined by the state of his consciousness, and one's consciousness is made up of all that he is – all that he thinks, believes, feels, hopes and does?"* So true, isn't it?

This gifted sense of intuition has been with us since birth, but most of us have not been aware of it, except for an occasional 'hunch' or two. To realize that such a powerful force exists within each of us usually takes much investigation, dedication and persistence.

So again, we need to look within to find that celestial spark which, when found, will *ignite* our lives.

As a bonus to this process, we will find that we can command the subconscious and it will faithfully carry out our orders. For it to do this, however, we must be absolutely sincere, and believe wholeheartedly in its innate capability. When we do, we will see some surprising results.

To prove this to yourself, declare to your subconscious mind as you retire that you want to get up at 6 o'clock the next morning. Picture the clock with its hands at 6 o'clock. Be sincere and authoritative about it, and do not rely on any alarm clock as a backup. When you awaken in the morning, you will find that your bedroom clock will register exactly 6 o'clock. Your inner clock has ticked off the correct amount of hours. Nobody knows just how this marvelous timepiece works. It is one of humanity's distinctive and intangible gifts.

Presupposing that your subconscious can do this, just imagine how many more fabulous things it can do for you! After all, it regulates all the functions of the body, so you know that it is a marvelous mechanism.

You are already saying, "You mean to tell me that the subconscious can even tell time!" Preposterous, you say! Just you give it a try.

Murdo Macdonald-Bayne explains it this way: **"This subconscious mechanism functions through the lower brain, the cerebellum and the medulla; and also through the sympathetic nervous system controlled by the Infinite Intelligence. Therefore, your sympathetic nervous system is affected by your thinking, as well as the cerebro-spinal nervous system, which is but the elongation of the brain."**

Instead of trying to comprehend this technical definition, let us just try to understand the divine sonship of man ('man' is always used in the generic sense) by realizing that Christ, the Spirit of Truth, is our link with our Source. Thus we come to realize the import of the passage, **"I and my Father are One."**

This brings us to the conclusion that the Superconscious, the conscious and the subconscious are three parts of one WHOLE-one Creative, Universal, All-Encompassing Mind. Three-in-One, a Divine Trinity, or Tri-Unity, clearly reminding us of another perceptive statement of Jesus when asked by Thomas the way of salvation. Said Jesus simply, **"I am the Way, the Truth and the Life."**

How simple, yet profound!

In all this talk involving the mind, let us not forget the quintessential quality of *love.* Dr. Anthony declares rightly that *"Love is the attracting, uniting, harmonizing force of the Universe."*

In line with this thought, I urge you to read *"The Greatest Thing in the World"* by Henry Drummond, a Scottish evangelical writer, lecturer and scientist who thrilled a large audience with this lecture in 1887. His resulting booklet sold over 350,000 copies – a remarkable success for that time period. This essay also can be found in the book *"Treasures of the Kingdom"* by T. Everett Haare. This same book contains many other inspiring lectures by other Protestant, Roman Catholic and Jewish clerics.

Since it is a lengthy essay, you may want to skip it for now. I am giving you the highlights, so that you may get the main points of this lecture.

Here they are:

"Everyone has asked himself the great question of antiquity as of the modern world. What is the summum bonum – the supreme good? You have life before you. Once, only can you live it. What is the noblest object of desire, the supreme gift to covet?"

We have been accustomed to be told that the greatest thing in the religious world is Faith. That great word has been the keynote for centuries of the popular religion; and we have easily come to look upon it as the greatest thing in the world. Well, we are wrong. If we have been told that, we may miss the mark. "Here abideth faith, hope and love, and the greatest of these is love!" The greatest of these *is* love!"

Paul contrasts love with eloquence, he contrasts it with prophecy; he contrasts it with sacrifice and martyrdom. After contrasting it with all these things, Paul, in three very short verses, gives us an amazing analysis of what this supreme quality is.

What are the ingredients of this noblest of noble attributes? Patience, Kindness, Generosity, Humility, Courtesy, Unselfishness, Good Temper, Guilessness and Sincerity – these make up the supreme gift.

Where Love is, God is. He that dwelleth in Love dwelleth in God. God is Love. Here is the vision of a truly living spirit: 'I will pass through this world but once. Any good thing, therefore, that I can do, or any kindness that I can show to any human being, let me do it now. Let me not defer it or neglect it, for I shall not pass this way again.'

So much for the analysis of Love. Now the business of our lives is to have these things fired into our characters. That is the supreme work to which we need to address ourselves in this world, to learn Love; and how to really love.

To love abundantly is to live abundantly; and to love forever is to live forever. Hence, eternal life is inextricably bound up with Love. We want to live forever for the same reason that we want to live tomorrow. Why do you want to live tomorrow? It is because there is someone who loves you, someone you want to be with tomorrow, and to be with and to love back. To love is to live-it is the essence of living."

"Everyone that loveth is born of God."

Say often, **"I am growing in the consciousness of Universal Love."**

"To possess a healthy self-esteem, (or love) is not to be immune to the vicissitudes of life, or to the pain of struggle." So says Dr. Nathaniel Brandon in *"Honoring the Self"*. On page 97, he follows this thought with: **"Genuine self-esteem in not comparative or competitive. Neither is genuine self-esteem expressed by self-glorification at the expense of others, or by the quest to make oneself superior to others, or to distinguish others so as to elevate oneself....Self-esteem, therefore, is the reputation we acquire with ourselves....In human beings, joy in the mere fact of existing is a core meaning of healthy self-esteem. It is a state of one who is at war neither with self nor with others."**

Although this term 'self-esteem' gets bandied about with many shades of meaning, I consider the above essential in understanding this phenomenon, as you find it given by no less an authority than the above named Dr. Brandon, perceptive author and recognized psychologist.

After all, isn't it more intelligent to go through life loving oneself rather than demeaning oneself, or always being in conflict with one's own intimate entity?

In the Bible passage, *"Thou shalt love thy neighbor as thyself"* we see that benevolent self-love is therefore according to Biblical admonition. Since in reality we are all connected; to even love oneself takes on new meaning. If you have always put yourself down, or felt inferior, consider this new and rewarding approach. You will find it extremely beneficial.

"We ask ourselves, who am I to be brilliant, gorgeous, talented and fabulous? Actually, who are you NOT to be?" Marianne Williamson.

You will discover that the more you direct and rely on your subconscious mind-*your source of primeval intelligence-* the more you will begin to realize your true potential.

1. Pray to the Superconscious Mind for the correct guidance.
2. Use the conscious mind to program this information into the subconscious.
3. Command your subconscious with what you feel to be a true impression.

For the moment the important thing is to is to stay with your present task and at the same time perhaps you can brighten the day for someone you don't even know. Whatever lightness and brightness you can bring to alleviate the sordid and the tragic, which besets mankind, will elevate your perspective and bring you lasting benefits. The biggest disease this world suffers from is that of feeling unloved.   All humanity needs your elevating sprightliness.

"For those who bring sunshine to the lives of others cannot keep it from themselves."   Sir James Barrie, Scottish novelist, playwright, and creator of the ever-popular and world-renowned play, "Peter Pan."

Francois La Rochefoucauld makes this penetrating observation: *"When we are unable to find tranquility within ourselves, it is useless to seek it elsewhere."*

"BELIEVE IN YOURSELF TO THE DEPTHS OF YOUR BEING. NOURISH THE TALENTS YOUR SPIRIT IS FREEING. KNOW IN YOUR HEART WHEN THE GOING GETS SLOW THAT YOUR FAITH IN YOURSELF WILL CONTINUE TO GROW. DON'T FORFEIT AMBITION WHEN OTHERS MAY DOUBT. IT'S YOUR LIFE TO LIVE-YOU MUST LIVE IT THRUOUT. LEARN FROM YOUR ERRORS; DON'T DWELL IN THE PAST NEVER WITHDRAW FROM A WORLD THAT IS VAST. BELIEVE IN YOURSELF; FIND THE BEST THAT IS YOU. LET YOUR SPIRIT PREVAIL; STEER A COURSE THAT IS TRUE."

Everlasting thanks to my Creator

FOR THE *RENEWING* GIFTS OF THE **SPIRIT!**

M. Frazier Keables

PORT XIII

THIS IS YOUR LIFE! REJOICE IN IT!

THIS is my life. This **IS** my life. This is **MY** life. This is my **LIFE**!

No matter how you say it, as you discover its primordial magnificence dawning upon you, you will begin to realize, perhaps for the first time, that this miraculous, glorious and portentous gift is yours to activate with all its potential HERE and NOW! Are any of us actually aware of these latent and quiescent powers that lie within us?

The moment we enter this world we are the possessors of the greatest gift of all –the gift of LIFE! Rejoice in it. Nurture it. Strengthen it. Encourage it. Re-invigorate it. Value it. Protect it. And use it for greatness, no matter how insignificant you may feel at the present moment.

The more you come to sense and to realize the inestimable value and the supreme miracle of human life, the less your mind will be filled with destructive thoughts of depression which sometimes lead one to suicide.

The eminent psychologist William James counsels us to: *"Believe that life is worth living, and your belief will help create the fact."*

We must learn to love life as the great Polish-born American pianist, Arthur Rubinstein, observed: *"I have found that if you love life, life will love you back."* What a great equation for all of us to prove for our own utilization! His life was expressed beautifully in his famous musical renditions. And now it is *you* who are seeking out the melody of life by tuning in to the essences of the Universe.

What an exemplary creed Henry van Dyke gives us in this idealistic exposition: **"To be glad of life because it**

105

gives you the chance to love and to work and to play and to look up at the stars, to be satisfied with your possessions, but not contented with yourself until you have made the best of them; to despise nothing in this world except falsehood and meanness; and to fear nothing except cowardice; to be governed by your admiration rather than your disgust; to covet nothing that is your neighbor's except kindness of heart and gentleness of manners; to think seldom of your enemies, often of your friends; and to spend as much time as you can in God's great out-of-doors; these are the little guideposts on the footpaths to peace. This is peace of mind."

What an elevating and demonstrable philosophy for so many of us who seek here and seek there without any real sense of fulfillment! In the above is a proven formula for your own harmony, a quality sorely needed in this hectic world of rapid transition.

"From the viewpoint of our separate self and smaller will, it's normal to act on the basis of our own desires and preferences; when we surrender our smaller self and will to the guidance of a higher will and dedicate our actions for the highest good of all concerned, we feel an inspired glow at the center of life. Life is this simple: We are living in a transparent world, and God shines through in every moment. This is not just a fable or a nice story; it is living truth. God manifests everywhere, in everything. We cannot be without God. It's impossible. It's simply impossible." –Thomas Merton

Psychologist Claudius Naranjo has said: *"We are a part of the Cosmos, a tide in the ocean of life, a chain in the network of processes that do not either begin, or end, within the enclosure of our skins."* Can you fathom this larger concept, connecting all of us?

Sensing this underlying organic totality, Admiral Richard E. Byrd in his solo dog-sled trek to the South Pole, experienced this singular enlightenment: **"I could feel no doubt of man's oneness with the Universe. The conviction came that that rhythm was too orderly, too harmonious, too perfect, to be a product of blind chance-that, therefore, there must be purpose in the whole and man was part of that whole and not an accidental offshoot. It was a feeling that transcended reason, that went to the heart of man's despair and found it groundless. The universe was a cosmos, not a chaos, and man was as rightfully a part of that cosmos as were the day and the night."**

As we begin to comprehend this concept, we come to appreciate that we are in reality an offspring of the ever-present Universal Spirit, a creation of Love. Realizing this, we become eager to learn how best to develop our talents and abilities to fulfill our purpose in contributing to the Divine Design.

The great 16th century French essayist, Michel de Montaigne, emphasizes the importance of this vision thus: *"The great and glorious masterpiece of man is how to love with purpose."* When you do, life will take on a much nobler meaning for you and you will be happier at heart.

The famous Welsh poet, Gwenallt, expresses a simple philosophy of global understanding in this ancient ballad:

"GOD HAS NOT FORBIDDEN US TO LOVE THE WORLD,
AND TO LEAVE MAN AND ALL HIS WORKS;
(RATHER) TO LOVE THEM WITH ALL THE NAKED SENSES;
EVERY SHAPE AND COLOR, EVERY VOICE AND SPEECH.
THERE IS A ***SHUDDER*** IN THE BLOOD
WHEN WE SEE THE TRACE
OF HIS CRAFTSMAN'S FINGERS UPON THE WHOLE CREATION."

Doesn't this inspiring epic send your senses swirling, as you picture the import of this man's discerning concept and its ennobling effervescence?

The 19th century Irish poet and dramatist, Oscar Wilde, describes this transcendent view resplendently in this declaration: ***"Ah! Somehow life is bigger after all than any painted angel; could we but see the God within us!"***

For all of us are an "eachness" within the allness of God.

If we are to sense the rationale of all creation, it is paramount for us to recognize this requisite realization.

By now you and I have traveled through twelve significant chapters together and I sincerely hope that you have profited from your journey to each port of call. And since the number 13 has always been, whether by chance or design, a prominent factor in my life, I want to make this 'port' my finest and, of course, the most meaningful to you.

For most of us life is not a journey of jubilance, and it takes much objective thinking to turn the drab into the delightful.

Let me now ask you, "Are you beginning to lead a more fulfilling and rewarding life than when you first opened the book?"

Have you found proven ways to look at life from a brighter and more positive standpoint?

Even gaining this much is a giant stride for most of us.

Thomas Carlyle, 19th century essayist and historian, brings us this idealistic view: ***"Every day that is born into the world comes in like a burst of music and rings the whole day through; and you make of it a dance, a dirge, or a lifemarch, as you will."*** In our mornings most of us are not inclined (and don't have the time) to give much thought to the kind of a day we will experience. But, why not make it *ring?*

Let's think about this now from Dr. Paul Johannes Tillich: ***"Where there is joy, there is fulfillment; and where there is fulfillment there is joy."***

That makes sense. One definition of 'joy' is fullness of heart. If your heart (your whole being) is filled with joy, then how can iniquity enter in? A full container cannot absorb more than its capacity.

In his challenging book, *"You Can Have It All"* Arnold L. Patent makes this startling statement: ***"Remind yourself that only one feeling is real – JOYFULNESS!"*** (Can this postulate be true with so much misery and violence all around us?)

If you cannot accept the above as a premise, then let's go for this one by Joseph Marmion: ***"Joy is the echo of God's life within us."*** Proving it is our intuitive self which senses true joy.

As we adopt this larger perspective, we are strengthened to keep our life on track and are better prepared to face up to the contradicting evidence we observe, and find many of our problems falling into a more manageable category.

Reinforcing this cheerful perspective is Brown Landone's re-discovery of the ancient Pythagorean Philosophy of Numbers which brought to him this momentous verity: **"To live and enjoy life is the one end of man! Once you recognize this truth, all of life will be transformed for you. Christ made this clear. He taught that He is Life; and that He came to earth so that His joy may be fulfilled in us! This is man's purpose on earth. All else are trivialities."**

Radiance and joyfulness are the rewards of the truly insightful individual, as the Greek philosopher Plutonius observes: *"There is always radiance in the soul of man, untroubled like the light in a lantern amid a wild turmoil of wind and tempest."*

Let us seek out that radiance, for, as it says in Ecclesiastes: *"Gladness of the heart is the life of man, and the joyfulness of a titan prolongeth his days."*

And just how do we achieve this happiness?

Georges Sand, 19th century French novelist gives us this recipe: *"One is happy as a result of one's own efforts….Happiness is no vague dream, of that I am sure."*

Here, then, are the ancient keys to developing a much happier and more dynamic outlook. Use these keys to unlock a brighter, more rewarding life for yourself and for those around you.

Remember to laugh often….laughing is so beneficial. The wisdom of Proverbs 17:22 is eternally true: *"A merry laugh doeth good like a medicine."*

The Japanese version is: *"Time spent laughing is time spent with the gods."*

In the medical pages of the Nov. '94 *"Ladies Home Journal"* is this up-to-date endorsement of such a remedy:

"Laughter may turn out to be the best medicine after all. Recent research has shown that in addition to lifting one's spirits, letting out a good guffaw actually helps boost the cardiovascular, muscular, respiratory and immune systems.

According to William Fry, M.D., and emeritus associate clinical professor of psychiatry at Stanford Medical School, healthy laughing is a type of light aerobic exercise – it increases a person's breathing rate, which increases the oxygen in the blood and stimulates muscles throughout the body. In one of Dr. Fry's studies, laughter temporarily raised participants blood pressure – beneficial because it increases circulation and, consequently, the distribution of nutrients to the body's tissues. In another study, laughter was found to boost the immune system; an analysis of participants blood showed increased activity of white blood cells which fight disease.

Fry says everyone can benefit from a hearty laugh. He suggests that people identify what best tickles their funny bone and actively seek it out." C.F.

Now that's a doctor's order that's easy to take!"

Find something to laugh at even if it's only yourself.

Douglas Jerrold notes in his *"The Future of Freedom"* that *"Humor is the harmony of the heart."* And humor is the sidekick of that superlative of human endowments – JOY!

Is such an attitude too much of a Pollyanna approach to life when we are surrounded by so much negativity?

Probing and logical questions………

To achieve such an optimistic frame of mind we will need to develop a calming perspective on life in general, a quality not easy to achieve.

To aid you in this endeavor, do this:

1. Start each morning by thanking God for whatever blessings do come to mind.
2. Maintain an inviolable attitude toward all violent and tragic events, the number of which is incalculable.

Even though you now see the feasibility and advantages of bringing more joy into your life, you are still puzzled as to how to effectively bring it about.

3. Try doing an unexpected kindness for someone.
4. Try treating others as you would like to be treated.
5. Rely on your intuition to guide you into many other ways to not only bring joy into your own life, but, incidentally, into the lives of those you meet along life's highway.

As you express joy in your everyday life, it will radiate to others and will result in your becoming a much happier person. As you feel the joyful essences of life, you will be lifted out of debilitating boredom.

Just think of how much *happier* persons can brighten up this old world of ours, and you decide right now to be one of them!

At the entrance to the gym at the University of Maine are these challenging words by Dr. Paul Dudley White, the famous heart specialist who endorsed bicycle riding as the ideal exercise: ***"Isn't it fascinating to know that it is possible to grow healthier as we grow older, instead of*** *expecting the reverse?"* What a tradition-breaking and inspiring revelation!

Recent discoveries in the field of nutrition are enabling many of us to live beyond the accepted span of years. Read up on Chinese, Amish, or other folk-honored methods of using herbal or other natural remedies. These are remedies which have proven effective over the centuries, so open your eyes to alternative therapy.

From time to time little-known secrets of health and longevity surface from the Himalayan region. If you are a seeker after esoteric knowledge, check out *"The Fountain of Life"* by Peter Kelder.

"Ageless Body, Timeless Mind" is another great book by the renowned Dr. Deepak Chopra.

Open your eyes now to the enlivening proposition that it was *human race consciousness*, and not God, which created old age in the first place. Let us think of age, then, not so much as a matter of time, as an experience in time. The effects of the years on the physical body depend not so much upon the physiology of the body, but rather on the psychology involved in your outlook. Let us then decide not to accept this time-worn, albeit universal, belief as inevitable, but instead look forward to more productive years as we grow more mature.

In *"The Amazing Results of Positive Thinking"* Norman Vincent Peale gives us a remarkable example of someone who did this: **"When he became 45, he stopped counting the years. Aging is often a matter of the spirit. It exists in the imagination before it exists in the body. It is in the mind. You can apply this same principle to sleep. You get little sleep one night and therefore you think you must be tired, but if a situation came along in which you were asked to do something you enjoyed, you**

would see how long the weariness would last. You saw
how quickly your imagination changed the way you felt.
Change the image of yourself. See yourself well,
observing the rules of good health and you will tend to
become that which you visualize and practice."

Remember there is a resistless circulation of all good
things through your life; and this resistless circulation
includes your body and all its rightful functions.

Keep your body cells encouraged and uplifted. Praise
them –give them a program of youth and virility (to you
ladies, youth and beauty), and they will build you a body of
which you can be eternally proud. Even though our body
cells are being constantly used up, these cells are being
replaced by new ones as we speak.

So, let's give ourselves a sense of celebration, enjoying
the full wonderment that we are ALIVE! Being ever
grateful for this pulsing, synchronized body of ours,
endeavoring to keep it finely tuned. And let us do as we
are advised in 1st Cor. 6:20 to **"Glorify God in your body
and in your spirit which are God's."** *KEY*

As Roy L. Smith says: *"Think of your life in terms of
eternity, and life will expand on your hands."*

May we celebrate this awareness right now by blessing
our family, our friends, our co-workers, God's beautiful
flowers and all the outpourings of Nature!

The rhythm of life is ever-present, if we could but sense
its melody.

Our Native Americans sensed it in their way of life.
Here is what Chief Seattle said in a letter to President
Franklin Pierce: **"There is no quiet place in the white
man's cities. No place to hear the leaves of Spring, or
the rustle of the insect's wings....the white man does not
seem to notice the air he breathes. Like a man dying for**

many days, he is numb to the stench. What is man without the beasts? If all the beasts were gone, men would die from the great loneliness of spirit; for whatever happens to the beasts also happens to man. All things are connected. Whatever befalls the earth befalls the sons of earth."

These primitive people sensed a unity, a purpose, a comprehensiveness of life which most of us today can barely fathom.

William Wordsworth, 18th century English poet, gives us this penetrating observation: *"With an eye made quiet by the power of harmony, and the deep power of joy, we see into the life of things."*

Let us then remember with Anne Morrow Lindbergh that: *"It is not the stony wildness that cuts you off from the people you love; it is the wildness in the mind, the desert wastes in the heart through which one wanders lost and is a stranger."*

We want to dispense with this 'wildness' and make these 'desert wastes' bloom.

Paul Tournier, M.D., from his experienced practice of medicine, is of the firm belief that every act of physical, psychological, or moral disobedience of God's purpose is an act of wrong living and has its inevitable consequences; thus leading to the foregone conclusion that man does not die; he actually kills himself.

In view of this dilemma, let us encompassingly reassure ourselves with this verse from Ez. 18:32 and recognize its implication:

"For I have no pleasure in the death of him that dieth, saith the Lord, *wherefore turn yourselves and live ye."*

Yes, *"turn"* and *"live."*

115

Turn now to your intuitive path wherein you will find enrichment, fulfillment and fun. Yes, fun! The kind of fun we enjoy when we have come through our learning experience and now feel capable of bucking up against the almost insuperable odds which so often beset us in our drive toward our own personal evolvement.

Imbibe these valuable truths, as enunciated below:

In 1695 Sir William Penn, British Admiral and the founder of the Commonwealth of Pennsylvania, had this to say: ***"The truest end of life is to know that life never ends."***

"For the law of the Spirit of Life in Christ Jesus hath made me free from the law of sin and death." Rom. 8:2

Reinforcing this declaration, Prov. 12:28 tells us: ***"In the pathway of righteousness is life, and in the pathway thereof there is no death!"***

Therefore erase all the old, negative tapes and record the new, positive affirmations of Christian belief.

God IS, therefore I AM!

"For we know that the Son of God has come and has given us an understanding, that we know Him who is true, and we are in Him who is true, in His Son, Jesus Christ. This is the true God and *eternal* Life."

And Jesus has declared; ***"I am the Way, the Truth, and the Life."***

By understanding that the 'Way' means following Jesus' precepts, and that this 'Way' is the essential 'Truth', you begin to comprehend the basis for your developing conviction that life is, and must be Eternal. As you gain this larger perspective, you discern the possibility –in fact- the imperative need- of extending your own life on this earth Here and Now!

What are Jesus' precepts?   In a nutshell they are twofold:

1.*You shall love the Lord your God with all your heart, with all your mind and with all your soul.*

2. You shall love your neighbor as yourself.

These two simple commands eloquently cover the elementary imperatives for a joyful and productive life.

Ten to one, you are not going to carry out all of the specifics you are reading about. But please do savor the stimulus of your improved optimistic outlook as you contemplate the endless possibilities ahead and become enraptured with your *new* potential.

"For you are no longer a servant, but a son, and if a son (or a daughter) then an heir of God." Gal. 4:7

The above are the great verities we need to magnify in our own lives so that others may see the multiple benefits of a truly genuine and more meaningful existence, and that we, ourselves, may finally grasp the reality of the eternality of life.

The more we perceive these precepts, the more we will find ourselves expressing the ebullience of God which is all around us, but how seldom do we realize it.

At this point we hear Voltaire, the 18th century French philosopher, historian, dramatist and essayist, instructing us in this manner: *"Let us read and let us dance – two amusements that will never do any harm to the world."*

So, come out of your shell and **SMILE! LAUGH! SING! DANCE!** and **SHOUT!** for **JOY!** It won't hurt a bit.

And don't let anyone steal your thunder!

It is time now to go from despair to hope, from hope to faith, and from faith to demonstration, having now discovered that life is no more aimless and meaningless, but can be purposeful and rewarding; and that as a unique individual, no matter how humble, you have an impelling function in life – perhaps even a great and noble one.

I urge you to evaluate the eternal verities presented here and to enrich your life with these invaluable treasures which can dynamically ***renew*** your mind and your body.

Discover your real potential NOW!

And **"*Renew* thyself completely each day. Do it again and again, and forever again!"**

BEHOLD!

THIS   IS   YOUR   LIFE!!!

ENJOY!   ENJOY!   ENJOY!

Author in 92nd year, June 2002

"YOUR HAPPINESS IS INTERTWINED
WITH YOUR OUTLOOK ON LIFE!"

AUTHOR'S NOTE

A direct descendant of John Robinson, the Pastor to the Pilgrims in Holland, the author wants you to find in this book that same special individual freedom which those devout souls were seeking.

Having spent many years collecting notes from the most advanced exponents of applied psychology and from the Scriptures, on a certain day a powerful intuition welled up in him and he felt impelled to write this book.

Once started, the words and the inspiration flowed in enabling him to fashion this interwoven garment out of the fabric at hand.

You will find this guidebook to be a basic instruction manual about capturing and applying that elusive faculty we call mind-power, aspiring to the achievement of a more positive outlook, and about the expostion of those basic truths which have been handed down through the ages by the world's greatest sages.

Knowingly or unknowingly, we are all seeking that mental, physical, and spiritual freedom which will give new purpose to our lives.

You will find this book rewarding reading, even if you feel that some of the things are not for you.

As the French say: BON LISANT!!!

Think of this book as the epitome of the Celebration of Life!

BIBLIOGRAPHY

Page 4 Vernon Howard—Perm. Of Pub. Parker Pub. & Simon & Schuster

Pages 6&36 Dyer: Per. Of Pub. Harper Collins

Page 7 Mann: Permission of Author

Pages 23, 27, 40, 45, 47, 66, & 77 Anthony: Permission of author

Page 23 Edwards, Permission of Pub. Wilshire Publishing

Page 24, 38, 49, 50, 57, 60, & 81 Per. Of Pub. Prentice Hall

Page 24 Smedley: Permission of Toastmasters International

Page 24, 25, 81 & 96 Peale: Permission of Peale Center

Pages 35, 58, 60 & 62 Roman: Permission H.J. Kramer

Pages 37, 59 & 60 Clarke: Permission of Author

Pages 37, 38: Swindoll, 1st Evangelical Free Church, Fullerton, CA

Pages 38, 39: Valoskovic: Per. Scripps-Howard News Service

Page 40 Bristol: Prentice-Hall

Pages 40, 47 Buscaglia: Pub. Slack, Inc.

Pages 41, 46, 48, 58, 59, & 81 Murphy, Pub. Simon & Schuster

Page 55 Schuller: Crystal Cathedral Publications

Pages 62 & 65: Carrel, Permission Forward Movement Publications
Page 61 Russel: Permission of Pub. DeVors, Publications

Page 73 Walker: Permission DeMond Publishers

Pages 78, 79, Perm. Pubs. MacMillan & Co. & Winchester-Graham

Page 80 Howard, Permission of Author

Page 86 Brandon: Perm. Of Pub.: Putnam-Berkley Group

Page 85 Haare: Perm. Of Pub. T. Everett Haare
Page 92 Patent: Permission of Author

Page 94 Fry: Permission of Meredith Corp.

Page 94 Jerrold, Permission of Pub. Ayer Corp.

Page 97 Lindbergh; Permission of Pub. Pantheon Books